HAY HOUSE BASICS

LUCID DREAMING

❖ Also in the Hay House Basics series ❖

<u>Publishing in 2016</u>

LUCID DREAMING

A Beginner's Guide to Becoming Conscious in Your Dreams

CHARLIE MORLEY

HAY HOUSE

Carlsbad, California • New York City • London
Sydney •Johannesburg • Vancouver • New Delhi

First published and distributed in the United Kingdom by:
Hay House UK Ltd, Astley House, 33 Notting Hill Gate, London W11 3JQ
Tel: +44 (0)20 3675 2450; Fax: +44 (0)20 3675 2451
www.hayhouse.co.uk

Published and distributed in the United States of America by:
Hay House Inc., PO Box 5100, Carlsbad, CA 92018-5100
Tel: (1) 760 431 7695 or (800) 654 5126
Fax: (1) 760 431 6948 or (800) 650 5115
www.hayhouse.com

Published and distributed in Australia by:
Hay House Australia Ltd, 18/36 Ralph St, Alexandria NSW 2015
Tel: (61) 2 9669 4299; Fax: (61) 2 9669 4144
www.hayhouse.com.au

Published and distributed in the Republic of South Africa by:
Hay House SA (Pty) Ltd, PO Box 990, Witkoppen 2068
Tel/Fax: (27) 11 467 8904
www.hayhouse.co.za

Published and distributed in India by:
Hay House Publishers India, Muskaan Complex, Plot No.3, B-2,
Vasant Kunj, New Delhi 110 070
Tel: (91) 11 4176 1620; Fax: (91) 11 4176 1630
www.hayhouse.co.in

Distributed in Canada by:
Raincoast Books, 2440 Viking Way, Richmond, B.C. V6V 1N2
Tel: (1) 604 448 7100; Fax: (1) 604 270 7161; www.raincoast.com

A catalogue record for this book is available from the British Library.

ISBN: 978-1-78180-343-1

Printed and bound by CPI Group (UK) Ltd, Croydon, CR0 4YY

For my teacher, Akong Rinpoche (1939–2013),
a man of few words, who once told me,
'Lucid dreaming? Yes, learn the
basics, that is best.'

For information about Akong Rinpoche's humanitarian
projects around the world, see www.rokpa.org

Contents

Lucid Dreaming Toolboxes

Introduction

It all started a couple of months before my 12th birthday. It was a Sunday afternoon and I was bored – as 11-year-olds often are when it's raining, it's Sunday and there's nothing to do. I started sifting through the weekend newspapers, looking for the mail-order gadgets brochure. Once I'd found it I spotted a full-page advertisement for something called a 'NovaDreamer', a computerized sleep mask that helped induce lucid dreams. As soon as I read about lucid dreaming something clicked, and I called out: 'That's so cool! Dad, I know what I want for my birthday!'

I never did get the NovaDreamer, but the seed had been planted nonetheless, and it began to sprout a few years later when I became fascinated with lucid dreaming once more and decided to learn how to do it.

When I became a teenager, the free accessibility of lucid dreaming was one of its major selling points. There was no equipment to buy, no initiation to be done, no club to join. The only requirements were sleep and determination. Also, it was a great place to have lots of dream-sex, which, as a teenager, seemed like a very good reason to learn how to lucid dream!

A few years later, when I got into Tibetan Buddhism, I started to learn about something called dream yoga. This is the term given to a collection of lucid dreaming, conscious sleeping, and what we in the West refer to as 'out-of-body experience' practices aimed at spiritual growth and mind training. Within the context of dream yoga the lucid dream state is used to go way beyond sexual fantasy – it's a way of doing spiritual practice while we sleep. At 19 years old I became captivated by this possibility.

Once my lucid dream practice became my spiritual practice things really started to take off. I spent the next five years reading everything I could find on both lucid dreaming and dream yoga. I received teachings on these practices from the rare few who were offering them, and went on Buddhist retreats with dream yoga specialists such as Lama Yeshe Rinpoche – the man who would eventually suggest that I start sharing my experiences with others. Lucid dreaming soon became an essential element of my spiritual path.

But how does all this relate to *you*? Well, after more than six years of teaching and 15 years of practice I can now confirm with certainty what I've always believed: lucid dreaming can change your life.

We sleep for a third of our lives and through lucid dreaming we can start to make use of that 30-year blackout for psychological and spiritual growth. What better practice could there be for today's busy lifestyles? We don't all make time for meditation every day, but almost everybody goes to sleep every night and so lucid dreaming is always accessible – it's the meditation practice you can do in your bed. That's some pretty effective time management.

But how does lucid dreaming actually benefit us? So many psychological problems have their source in the fact that we don't know ourselves. We don't know our minds; we're often unmindful and unaware. Through lucid dreaming we get to truly know ourselves, and to become more mindfully aware in all states of day and night.

Our unconscious minds hold a wealth of wisdom – both about ourselves and the world around us. This treasure trove is rarely accessed in the waking state but once we become lucid we gain access to a library of insight that resides in our dreaming mind. Through lucid dreaming we become conscious *within* the unconscious. This opens up the possibility of directly communicating with our own divine potential, and witnessing just how limitless we actually are.

Studies from Harvard University in the USA concluded that most people are unaware and not in the present moment for 47 per cent of their lives.[1] Through lucid dreaming we can change that statistic, for lucidity in our dreams leads to lucidity in life. We can learn to 'wake up' in our daily lives, just as we can in our dreams. Bringing lucid awareness into even just a few moments of our nightly blackout is such a powerful de-conditioning tool that it can lead to a remarkable enhancement of clear-seeing awareness while we're awake. Suddenly, we find ourselves lucid in situations that we'd usually sleepwalk through.

We wake up to our negative projections, our doubts and our illusory limitations. We begin to dream our destiny into existence by becoming the full potential of what we could be, if only we dared to dream.

So, fluff up that pillow, get ready for bed and buckle up, because you're in for a ride.

Author's note

If you're looking for an in-depth exploration of lucid dreaming within the context of Tibetan Buddhism and mindfulness meditation, you might prefer my first book for Hay House, *Dreams of Awakening*, but if you're after a light-hearted guide to the 'how, why and wow!' of lucid dreaming then you have the perfect book in your hands!

In *Dreams of Awakening* I used my own dreams to explore the ways in which lucid dreaming can be used on the spiritual path, but in this book you'll find as case studies the uncensored dream reports and reflections of some of the people I've had the privilege to teach.

Many of the techniques included in this book can also be found in *Dreams of Awakening*, in a more detailed form. Here they've been made more concise and accessible for the beginner lucid dreamer, but they still pack all the punch they need to bring you to fully conscious awareness within your dreams.

Part 1
THE BASICS

'All human beings are also dream beings.
Dreaming ties all mankind together.'
Jack Kerouac

Chapter 1
Control freaks, icebergs and unopened mail

So what is lucid dreaming? It's the art of becoming conscious within your dreams. A lucid dream is one in which you think, *Aha! I'm dreaming!* while you're still asleep. Once you become conscious within a dream, you can interact with and direct it at will, dancing with your unconscious mind.

If you have any interest in psychology, mindfulness, imagination, or the power of the unconscious, you'll love lucid dreaming. It allows you conscious access to the deepest depths of your mind, and the opportunity to guide your dreams at will.

How does lucid dreaming work?

In a lucid dream you've not woken up - in fact, you're still sound asleep - but part of the brain has reactivated (the right dorsolateral prefrontal cortex, in case you're wondering), allowing you to experience the dream state consciously with self-reflective awareness. Once you know that you're dreaming *as* you're dreaming, you gain access to the most powerful virtual-reality generator in existence: the human mind.

For me, one of the most revolutionary aspects of lucid dreaming is that it makes sleep fun! It completely reconfigures our relationship with the third of our lives that we spend in bed. Suddenly, sleep is not just 'wasted time', as some people see it, but rather a potential training ground for psycho-spiritual growth and a laboratory of internal exploration that makes us more lucidly aware in our waking lives too. Once we become conscious within our unconscious, we see that we're limitless, boundless and creative beyond our wildest imaginings.

Most people have had a lucid dream at some point in their lives, but through the process of learning the art of lucid dreaming we can come to experience this amazing phenomenon intentionally and at will. In fact, the term 'lucid dreaming' is a bit of a misnomer – it should really be 'conscious dreaming', because it's the aspect of conscious awareness that defines the experience, rather than its lucid clarity, but for now we'll stick with it.

However, given that there's so much misunderstanding around what lucid dreaming actually *is*, it's worth taking a moment to look at what lucid dreaming is *not*...

❖ It's *not* a half-awake/half-asleep state. In a lucid dream you're in REM (rapid eye movement) dreaming sleep and out for the count, but part of your brain has become reactivated while you're dreaming, allowing you to experience the dream consciously.

❖ It's *not* just a very vivid dream – although lucid dreams are often super-vivid, high-definition experiences.

❖ It's *not* an out-of-body experience (sometimes called astral projection). This point is still being debated by many lucid dreaming practitioners, but as I see it, a lucid dream happens primarily within our own personal mindstream, whereas in an out-of-body experience we move beyond these boundaries.

Lucid dreaming *is* a dream in which you know you're dreaming *as* you're dreaming. I'm glad we've cleared that up!

Once lucid, you become fully conscious within a three-dimensional construct of your own mind. You can literally walk – or fly – around a projection of your own psychology and have complex, involved conversations with personifications of your own psyche.

With high level lucidity comes high level clarity of mind. This means you can reflect on the fact that you're asleep and that your body is lying in bed. You can think to yourself, *Wow this is so cool, I can't wait to tell people about this when I wake up!* and you can access your waking memories and personal experience. It's *you* in there, but that you is limitless. This means you can heal, meditate and learn in ways that might seem impossible in the waking state.

That's pretty far out, but it's not the *most* far out thing by a long way. What really shocks most newbie lucid dreamers is how *real* it feels. A lucid dream looks, feels, tastes and smells as real as waking reality and yet it's primarily a projection of the mind. If you're struggling to imagine just how a lucid dream feels, check out the dream reports in the case studies throughout the book. Page 37 is a good one to start with.

And for any sceptics or naysayers out there, know this – lucid dreaming is for real. It has been a scientifically verified phenomenon of dreaming sleep for almost 40 years. It exists, and we know this because it has unique and 'discernable neural correlates', which means that it's not just psychological, it's physical.

The science bit

In 2009, researchers at Frankfurt University's neurological clinic confirmed that 'lucid dreaming constitutes a hybrid state of consciousness with definable and measurable differences from the waking state and from the REM (rapid eye movement) dream state.'[1] Then in 2012, at Munich's Max Planck Institute of Psychiatry, it was discovered that when lucid consciousness was attained within the dream, activity in 'brain areas associated with self-assessment and self-perception, including the right dorsolateral prefrontal cortex and frontopolar regions, increase markedly within seconds.'[2]

How did they discover this? If you hook someone up to brain-monitoring equipment such as EEG, or a functional magnetic resonance imaging (fMRI) device – a type of scanner that uses magnetic resonance imaging to create a live picture of the brain's activity – and watch them dream, you'll see that the brain stem and occipital lobe in the back part of the brain become highly active, whereas the very front part of the brain, the prefrontal cortex, is almost entirely inactive.

Scientists believe that the personality centres[3] and the sense of self originate in areas in the prefrontal cortex,[4] so, as these areas of the brain are 'offline' while we dream,[5] we can happily accept that we really are, say, the queen of Egypt. Until we wake up, our prefrontal cortex comes back 'online' and we realize that being the queen of Egypt was just a dream.

But in a lucid dream a different process occurs. When we become lucid, areas in the prefrontal cortex switch back on while we're still dreaming, and so we think, *Hang on, queen of Egypt?... I must be dreaming!* Or, in the poetic terms of meditation expert Rob Nairn: 'Once we realize that what we thought was real is actually a dream we experience a direct shift in consciousness. And so the labyrinthine psyche is revealed to us.[6]

One of the most common entries into a spontaneous lucid dream is spotting a dream 'anomaly' and realizing that you must be dreaming. How does this work? You're dreaming away when something weird happens and you think, *What the...? This can't happen in real life, I must be dreaming!*

For many beginner lucid dreamers, this leads to a rush of adrenaline – *Wow, this is amazing!* – and the next thing they know they're awake in bed, heart pounding, buzzing with excitement from their first lucid dream. With practice, however, it's possible to stay in the lucid dream for as long as we like – we'll look at how to do this later.

Strange but true

If it feels as if you've been in a lucid dream for five minutes, you probably have. Research has shown that for most people the experience of time in the lucid dream state is roughly the same as in the waking state.[7] Why? Because once lucid, we have much the same ability to estimate time as we do when awake. Imagine spending an hour (the length of your longest dream period) exploring the inside of your own mind.

Will lucid dreaming make me tired?

No, it won't – in fact most people wake up feeling much more refreshed from lucid dreams than from everyday, non-lucid ones. Lucid dreaming occurs almost exclusively within REM dreaming sleep, which is not actually a restful sleep state. In fact, the original name for REM sleep was 'paradoxical sleep' – the paradox being that the brain is often more active during dreaming than it is while we're awake.

Every stage of sleep has a purpose. The non-REM and deep sleep stages that make up the majority of our sleep are needed primarily to rest the body and 'clean the brain',[8] whereas the REM dreaming stages are needed to reconsolidate our memory and integrate our psychological processes.

Non-lucid dreaming does this naturally, of course, but once we become lucid within our dreams the brain has sometimes been observed to start exhibiting high-frequency gamma brain waves, which have been linked to high-level meditation,[9] hypnosis and psychological growth. This may mean that, once lucid, the REM dreaming stage becomes *even more* beneficial than usual.

Also, for most people, lucid dreaming holds such a buzz of excitement that the day after a lucid dream will often be lit up with a sense of joy and achievement.

Realer than real

As I mentioned earlier, the weird thing about lucid dreams is that they're often not very dreamlike at all. Fully lucid dreams can seem so completely realistic that many people believe they've entered another dimension of reality. In fact they have – but the dimension is not out in space somewhere, it's in the space inside their mind.

The sophisticated detail of the lucid dream is outstanding. Put your hand on your heart and often you'll be able to feel it beating, even though both your heart and your hand are all simply the stuff that dreams are made of. A lucid dream can feel even realer than real life, and this hyperreality comes from the fact that our senses are not limited to the constraints of the physical sense organs. For example, my eyesight was once quite poor in real life[10] and yet perfect in the lucid dream. This is because, in the lucid dream, I wasn't seeing through my eyes, I was seeing through my mind.

However, although the lucid dream world may *look* similar to the waking world, the same rules do not apply. This means that we can fly, teleport, communicate telepathically with dream characters and guide the narrative of the dream with our will and expectation. In fact, the lucid dream is a meticulously intricate mental construct that may seem so real that we come to question the very nature of waking reality.

So does this mean that lucid dreamers stand to lose touch with what's real? No, in fact quite the opposite happens. Once we can see through the hallucinatory reality of the dreamscape, and know it as illusion, we become better equipped to recognize illusion in the waking state. This makes us more mentally stable and self-aware.

Strange but true

Dream researcher Jayne Gackenbach references a subject who used lucid dreaming to lose weight. The report shows that the woman would refrain from eating fatty foods during the day because she knew she could eat them in her dreams. Perhaps eating food in a lucid dream is so realistic that the brain sends satiation signals to the gut saying, 'I'm full'. Hypnotic gastric band eat your heart out!

Trying to explain how lucid dreaming *feels* is like trying to describe the taste of chocolate. I can use all the adjectives under the sun but at no point will you truly *know* what chocolate tastes like until you actually eat some. So it is with lucid dreaming. This book will help you taste the chocolate. In fact, when people first start reading about lucid dreaming, they often start to smell the cocoa and realize they *have* had lucid dreams, and that they too can find the golden ticket for a visit to the chocolate factory.

Controlling the dream

Once you're lucid you can actually *choose* what to do in your dream. This can be anything from going surfing to meditating within the dream or meeting a personification of your higher self, but many beginners choose to fly. They become lucid, set their intention to fly, and then zoom off over the dreamscape, controlling their speed and trajectory as they go. This degree of subjective control may well lead them to believe that they're controlling the whole dream, but this is simply not the case.

In his book *Lucid Dreaming: Gateway to the Inner Self* lucid dreaming expert Robert Waggoner said: 'No sailor controls the sea. Similarly, no lucid dreamer controls the dream.' This is very true, for just as it would be an arrogant sailor who believed that he was controlling the awesome power of the sea, so it is with our dreams.

To think that our paper-tiger ego (which we bring into the dream once lucid) can in any way control or dominate the awesome power of the unconscious is to attribute to it an inflated degree of influence. The unconscious dreaming mind is so much more powerful than the ego-mind, and lucid dreamers who believe they can control the dream have vastly underestimated what they're dealing with.

To aim at control is often to subjugate, to dominate and to suppress – so, rather than control, let's aim to choreograph, influence and direct the dream. I know it's more a matter of semantics than anything else, but words have a powerful effect on the unconscious, so be mindful of the energy that your words contain. We must make an ally of our unconscious, not an enemy. Don't try to control your dreaming mind – instead, try to befriend it, because once you've made a friend of your unconscious you'll have access to more energy than you ever thought possible.

Strange but true

It seems that playing videos games can be good for lucid dreaming (sorry, parents!). Dream psychologists have reported that 'gamers who are used to controlling their game environments can translate that into their dreams.'[11] Research shows that people who frequently play video games are more likely to have lucid dreams, and they are also better able to influence their dream worlds once lucid.

Creating new pathways in the brain

We've long been told that 'you can't teach an old dog new tricks', but a wonderfully optimistic finding from neuroscience, called neuroplasticity, is asking us to rethink the outdated idea that the brain's physical structure is unchangeable once we reach adulthood. Neuroplasticity is a term that refers to the brain's ability to change and adapt in response to newly learned or repeated actions, and it can be engaged through lucid dreaming.

How? Our neurological system doesn't differentiate between our waking experiences and our lucid dream experiences, which means that for our brain dreaming lucidly about doing something isn't like *imagining* it – it's like actually *doing* it. The lucid dream is so visceral that the brain will start to function in accordance with what we're dreaming about. Ultimately, this means that you can *learn* in your lucid dreams, you can *train* in them, and you can even make lasting changes to the very fabric of your brain.

But how does this work? Thanks to the activation of the prefrontal brain areas that accompanies full lucidity, we can begin to engage the full potential of neuroplasticity while we sleep. During lucid dreams neural pathways in the brain can be strengthened and created, just as they can while we're awake. This means that dreamers who consciously engage in certain practices within their lucid dreams (such as sport, art or acts of kindness) are creating and strengthening the pathways associated with those practices, making them easier to do in the waking state.

Therefore, each time you act with courage in a lucid dream you're strengthening the neural pathways associated with courage in the waking state. And every time you extend the hand of friendship to your unconscious mind you're cementing a relationship that'll continue once you're awake.

In non-lucid dreams, neuroplasticity is not engaged to the same extent (so don't sweat that dream in which you throttled your boss!), but once we're lucid, and we can decide what to do, we can affect our neural pathways based on the actions we perform. The implications of this are huge – we can change our brain while we sleep.

The iceberg of the mind

Sigmund Freud, the father of psychoanalysis and author of *The Interpretation of Dreams*, did much to popularize the use of dream work in a therapeutic setting. Although many of his ideas seem quite dated today, his model of the psyche is as relevant now as it was 100 years ago.

Freud's theories led to imagining the mind like an iceberg, which, as we know, is much bigger below the surface than it is above it. This comparison formed the basis of Freud's distinction between the conscious and the unconscious mind. He believed that the immediately recognizable part of the mind, the 'conscious mind', is actually the much smaller aspect, and that the majority of the mind is 'unconscious' – the part hidden beneath the surface.

Many people believe that they're nothing more than what they're *conscious* of: their thoughts, feelings, beliefs and perceptions, but that's only a fraction of who they really are. Sadly, most of us sleepwalk through our lives, limited by what we can see floating on the surface and unaware of the powerhouse of mental energy that lies beneath.

The unconscious contains huge stores of information (everything we've ever done, said, heard or seen), to which the conscious mind has limited access in the waking state. Using this iceberg image we can imagine that about 10 per cent of our mind is conscious, observable and available to our rational waking awareness, whereas about 90 per cent of it is unconscious,[12] often unrecognized and made of seemingly irrational content – irrational to our conscious mind, that is.

So, what's one of the easiest ways to explore the unconscious? Through our dreams. Dreams are primarily created and sourced from the unconscious mind, so to explore our dreams is to explore our unconscious. Lucid dreaming takes this exploration a step further because, as hypnotherapy expert Valerie Austin once told me, it allows us 'access to this data straight from the unconscious without it being edited by our rational, conscious mind'.

Our true capacity is just waiting to be revealed to us, and when we start to do mind-training work such as meditation, self-hypnosis, energy work and, of course, lucid dreaming, we begin to get an idea of just how deep the iceberg goes.

Wanna go deeper?

So, if our mind is like an iceberg, what's the ocean in which it floats? And can we access that ocean from within our lucid dream? The answer is 'yes'. It seems that once we access the depths of the iceberg through our lucid dreams we can explore its outer reaches, which will bring us into contact with the transpersonal collective unconscious and beyond (more about this later).

With practice we can even leave the iceberg entirely, through the partially permeable membrane of the lucid dream, and explore the universal oceanic mind in which it floats. For more information about how this kind of out-of-body exploration works, check out my first book, *Dreams of Awakening*.

Collecting our post

It's been said that every time we dream our unconscious mind writes us a letter. Many of us don't bother to read these letters – and some of us are unaware that we're even receiving them – but everybody dreams, and so we're all receiving letters from our dreaming mind each night. Sometimes the letters are just summaries of the day's events but at other times they offer profound insights into our current mental state. Each letter is unique and each night offers new letters to read.

Imagine writing to a friend every night for their entire life, knowing full well that they aren't even collecting their post, let alone reading your letters. Nonetheless you tirelessly keep writing to them. Then one day you see that your friend is finally beginning to read your letters. How would that feel? You'd probably feel a joyous sense of connection to that friend you'd not felt before, and you might also begin writing more juicy, interesting and exciting letters. So it is with our dreams.

But how can we begin to read the letters from our unconscious, and to bear witness to what it's trying to communicate? We need to start collecting our post, which means that we need to start *remembering* our dreams. This not only offers you a valuable insight into the content and tone of your unconscious mind, but it also tells the unconscious that you're ready to listen to it. Suddenly the letter writer is being heard after all those years of being ignored. What joy! And now the unconscious wants to write more letters, of deeper significance this time, and to share more profound insights.

Meeting the letter writer

One day you decide that you'd like to meet your pen friend face to face, so you start practising the lucid dreaming techniques which makes that possible. That night, you find yourself fully lucid within your dream. The letter writer is busy writing away and then suddenly you walk into the dream while she's writing.

Imagine how pleased she'd be to see you! Imagine the conversation you'd have. Think of the friendship you could form. This is what happens when we become lucid within our dreams: we finally meet the letter writer face to face. But take heed, the letter writer has been writing to us for years and now that she finally has a chance to speak to us we can be sure that she won't bother with small talk – she may well get straight to the juicy bits. This is why our lucid dreams can be such intense, revealing experiences. We learn about aspects of our mind that have been hidden from view for so much of our life.

But let's not get ahead of ourselves. Before you meet the letter writer you need to start reading her letters. How? By training yourself to remember your dreams. Dream recall is not only the foundation of our relationship with our unconscious, it's also the foundation of our lucid dreaming practice. It's this foundation that we're going to lay now as we open up our first lucid dreaming toolbox and explore how to recall and document our dreams.

🧰 TOOLBOX 1: REMEMBER, REMEMBER

Dream recall is one of the most important aspects of lucid dream training. Some say that until you regularly remember your dreams you might be having lucid dreams every night without realizing it! Although that's a possibility, it's actually far more likely that if you don't remember your dreams you probably aren't going to have many lucid ones. Why? Because 'the more conscious you are of your dreams, the easier it will be to become conscious *within* your dreams'.[13]

Recalling and documenting your dreams

Most people have four or five dream periods every night, but not everybody remembers these. I believe the main reason is simply because we don't *try* to remember them.

At the first lucid dreaming workshop I ever ran, I met a gentleman who was convinced that he didn't dream because he hadn't remembered one in years. I tried to explain to him that everybody dreams, but he didn't want to hear it. However, after just one week of setting a strong intention to remember his dreams, he told me: 'Charlie, I realize that I've been dreaming for 62 years, I just never cared to notice!'

So, if we set a strong *intention* to recall our dreams, and if we 'care to notice', most of us will be able to recall at least *part* of them without too much difficulty after just a couple of nights. Here's how:

Five steps to boosting your dream recall

1. Set your intention to recall your dreams before you start dreaming. Before bed and even as you're falling asleep, recite over and over in your mind: *Tonight, I remember my dreams. I have excellent dream recall.*

2. If you want to remember your dreams, try waking yourself during a dream period so that the dream is fresh in your mind. How do we know when these occur? We'll learn more about this later, but the last two hours of your sleep cycle are when your longest dream periods occur.

3. Often, the memories of our dreams are felt in our bodies rather than our minds, so don't forget to explore any feelings in your body that you wake up with. Sometimes my recollection of a dream is as simple as: *Can't remember much of the dream but I woke with a feeling of happiness in my belly.*

4. If you can recall just one fact or feeling from your dream, you can work backwards from that point, eventually gathering the rest of the dream. As soon as you wake up, ask yourself some questions: *Where was I? What was I just doing? How do I feel?*

5. Don't give up on your dream if you can't remember it straight away. Often, my dreams come back to me while I'm having a cup of tea over breakfast, or sometimes even as late as the following afternoon when I become drowsy and my mind edges back to the dream state. Give yourself space to remember.

The most important of these five steps is the first one: as you fall asleep strongly set your intention to remember your dreams.

The next tool in our toolbox is a dream-work classic: the dream diary. Keeping a dream diary is simple – here's how to do it.

Keeping a dream diary

✦ Whenever you wake up from a dream, recall as much of it as you can and then write it down or document it in some way. You don't need to record every tiny detail – you'll know what feels worth noting and what doesn't.

✦ Focus on the main themes and feelings, the general narrative and any strange dream anomalies that you can recall. You're recording your dreams primarily so that you get to know the landscape, the atmosphere, and the 'territory' of your dreams (see toolbox 2 for more about this) – three aspects that will help you to recognize your dreams lucidly.

✦ You don't need to spend half an hour every morning documenting your dreams; in fact, you'll be surprised how much you write up in just five or 10 minutes. I rarely spend more than 10 minutes writing down my dreams at night, but I often expand them further over breakfast.

Many people like to type their dream recollections onto a tablet or a smartphone, while others like to use a notebook and pen. Either method is fine.

Strange but true

It seems that clean living might be able to help clean up our dream recall. Within the Tibetan dream yoga teachings the recipe for remembering your dreams is to 'avoid pollutions and impurities'. So a Big Mac before bed is off the menu, I'm afraid. Check out Chapter 6 for more on eating a dreamy diet.

. . . .

Sounds like hard work – do I have to?

Yes, you have to! Sorry. Best just to get on with it, because if you want to learn how to lucid dream properly then keeping a dream diary is *essential*.

Every time you write down a dream you reinforce the habit of viewing them as something valuable. Once you see dreams as valuable you'll naturally start to recall them with more ease. I advise that you even write an entry in your dream diary if you can't remember any dreams. 'Woke up with no dream recall' is still a valid dream diary entry and it'll help foster the habit of keeping a dream diary every night.

Besides, documenting your dreams is good for you! Don't just take my word for it – take dream work pioneer Carl Jung's, who believed that the beneficial integration of the unconscious happened primarily in our sleep, and that 'remembering dreams and writing them down' enhances this integration.[14]

And if you don't believe Jung then believe my mum. One of the most helpful things she ever did for me was to encourage me to tell her my dreams each morning. She knew that it was good for me, and although I didn't know it at the time she was helping me keep a kind of verbal dream diary throughout my formative years. This set me up with a pretty solid foundation in dream work that allowed me to start having spontaneous lucid dreams from the age of about seven.

I should say, though, that this wasn't because I was some sort of lucid dreaming prodigy – it was actually down to laziness. These childhood lucid dreams were mainly a result of my wetting the bed from within the dream, because I couldn't be bothered to wake up and use the toilet! I remember the feeling of a full bladder seeping into the dream and making me become fully lucid. Then, from within the dream, I would think to myself: *I really don't want to get out of bed to pee. Maybe I'll just do it while I'm still in the dream?*

Anyway, enough of me and my weirdly beneficial bed-wetting. Why do we have to keep a dream diary again? Because by recalling our dreams we're getting to know the territory of our dreaming mind, and the better we know that, the more likely we are to recognize it when we're in it and become lucid.

Okay. Got it. Anything else I should know?

Write down your dreams as soon as you remember them – yes, even if this is in the middle of the night. It's far better to write them down straight away because in the morning even the most memorable dream may well be forgotten.

I know it can seem pretty hectic, having to scrabble around for your dream diary at 5 a.m., but you'll soon find the least disruptive method for you. Whether it's going to the bathroom to write up your dreams or keeping a little torch by your bedside to avoid waking your partner, you'll find a way. Personally, I use my iPhone as my dream diary, because it lights up and because I can type into it faster than I can write. I then email myself the dreams and print them out at the end of each month.

Wanna go deeper?

Mind maps, illustrations, spider diagrams and artwork can all be incorporated into your dream diary. The important thing is to recall the dream – *how* you do it is secondary. You can even dance out your dreams. Once a year I run a 'Dance and Dreaming' retreat with the School of Movement Medicine in which we dance out our dreams each morning, using the dance floor as our dream diary.

Oh, and one more thing: I would advise against using voice recorders, unless you're super-mindful. Although it's difficult to 'sleep write', we can definitely 'sleep talk', so if you try to record your dream into a voice recorder when you're not fully awake, you may well end up with a recording of yourself falling asleep.

So that should be enough to get you started on recalling and documenting your dreams, but for those of you who want to step up a level, check out these tips from the king of dream recall and board member of the International Association for the Study of Dreams, Ryan Hurd.

Tips from the pros: Keeping a dream journal, with Ryan Hurd

❖ Keep the journal just for dreams, and for no other purposes – no recipes, phone numbers, to-do lists, or notes from class. Make sure the journal feels 'inviting'. It can be a fancy leather-bound one or just a spiral-bound notebook you picked up at the supermarket, but make sure you'll want to use it.

❖ Choose a special pen that's dedicated for use with the dream journal. Keep them together at all times.

❖ Keep the journal on your bedside table or close at hand when you go to bed. Notice it before you go to sleep and set an intention to use it.

❖ Keep a small reading lamp or torch close by, for when you wake in the middle of the night with a dream memory.

❖ Warn your partner. It's important that you feel you have social permission to turn on the light whenever you need to.

❖ If you're tech-savvy, try a dream journalling app on your tablet or smartphone. I recommend the apps by SHADOW, Dreamboard and DreamCloud.

❖ Journal immediately after you wake up, before getting out of bed. If you're pressed for time, make it easy on yourself and write down a few key phrases that'll jog your memory later.

❖ Personally, I use the present tense, as if the action is unfolding now.

❖ Don't lose heart. Be patient with yourself; it may take some time to fully reawaken the recall but it will happen.

❖ Reread your previous dreams from the night before as you settle down to sleep. You may be surprised that you remember more about the dream than you did when you first wrote it down.

Ryan Hurd is the author of *Dream Like A Boss,* and editor of the *Dream Studies Portal.* Visit www.DreamStudies.org for more of his dreamy advice.

CHARLIE'S TOOLBOX CHECKLIST ✍

- ❖ Set your intent to remember your dreams before you go to sleep.

- ❖ Document your dreams at least five nights out of seven (seven out of seven is best, of course, but life happens).

- ❖ Use whatever method you like (notebook/digital/artwork/dance) as a way to keep track of your dreams.

- ❖ Write down your dreams as soon as you remember them.

- ❖ Just five or ten minutes is sufficient time to spend writing down your dreams upon awakening.

- ❖ If you dream that you need to pee, make sure you wake yourself up #advicetomyyoungerself

Chapter 2
Sex, sport and psychological baggage

Engaging in sexual fantasy while lucid dreaming is extremely common and it isn't anything you need be ashamed of. In fact, Patricia Garfield, author of the classic *Creative Dreaming*, said that 75 per cent of her lucid dreams were either initiated by, or led to, orgasm or sexual activity of some sort. (Sounds great, but I don't think I could keep up, Pat.)

Sexual dreaming

For many novice lucid dreamers, sex is just part of the ride. Of course that's fine, but I always caution people not to get *too* much into this aspect, because although it can be a lot of fun, and it does feel incredibly realistic, it can become worryingly addictive, as I found out when I first started lucid dreaming in my teens.

By the age of 17, after months of lucid dream training, I started having regular lucid dreams and gained access to a virtual reality of incredible realism in which social norms didn't apply. Not yet aware of the Tibetan Buddhist lucid dream practices that I now teach, and at the peak of my wild teenage years, I didn't view the lucid dream state as a potential training ground for enlightened action. I saw it purely as a place to get laid.

Strange but true

A study by the University of Montreal in Canada investigating non-lucid dreams found that approximately 8 per cent of the dream reports contained some form of sexual activity. It also found that celebrities were twice as likely to be part of the female subjects' dream content, while multiple partners were reported twice as frequently in the male subjects' dreams.[1]

I'd trained myself to become the choreographer of my lucid dreams, and so I choreographed them to fulfil my desires. As my skills in lucid dreaming developed, I was soon able to make sexual partners manifest at will, and I even found myself going to bed early in order to meet up with the 'women of my dreams'. Sad but true.

This may all sound like harmless fun, but because of the phenomenon of neuroplasticity (see Chapter 1), I was creating strong neural pathways and habits associated with uncontrolled sexual hedonism, and these started to become activated in the waking state too. And so, inevitably, trouble lay ahead. In time, though, I realized that the potential of lucid dreaming was profound – and that it was a waste to spend it just having sex.

So, have fun with your practice, and if you want to have sex in your lucid dreams then go ahead, but try not to get stuck on the desire stage for too long. Although I believe that every lucid dream (whatever you use it for) is a potentially positive experience, there are definitely more psychologically beneficial things to do than have sex with your Self.

Strange but true

During some of the first scientific trials into lucid dreaming a Stanford University research team recruited a student volunteer called, appropriately enough, Randy, who was hooked up to a brain wave monitor and, more importantly, a penile strain gauge (don't ask), before being told to 'engage in sexual activity within the lucid dream'. All while being monitored by several members of the laboratory team.

The nocturnal mind gym

'Not enough time to play your favourite sport? Too tired to go to the gym after work? Want to maximize your athletic potential? Imagine if you could train in your sleep and actually improve your performance!' Although it sounds like an advertisement for a dubious weight loss scheme, it's actually quite possible. Following scientific studies conducted over the past 30 years, we now have persuasive evidence that practising sports *within* the lucid dream state can lead to remarkable increases in waking-state performance.

But how does this actually work? Research tells us that it's not only the case that 'in lucid dreams, athletes can explore more risky actions, practise without fear of injury, and develop greater creativity in sports',[2] but also that they can actually gain 'new sensory-motor skills' as they do it. Training while in the lucid dream state creates neural pathways that will carry over into the waking state, because, as we've learned, our neurological system doesn't differentiate between lucid dream and waking experiences.

But haven't athletes been using imaginary rehearsal for decades, visualizing the perfect performance as they sit on the sidelines? Yes, but the results from lucid dream training are much greater than those from imaginary rehearsal, because research shows that 'perception in lucid dreams is closer to waking perception than imagination'[3] and so the effectiveness of lucid dream practice is far greater than that of waking-state, imaginary rehearsal.

The scientists say that the main downside of waking visualization is that 'if the mental imagery technique is performed inadequately, without sufficient attention, subsequent gains in motor performance will be substandard'.[4] Lucid dreaming, however, solves this problem because it's the most comprehensive visualization possible and allows for the most complete realization of the technique.

The science bit

The scientists say that the reason we can increase our performance through mental practice is that 'the peripheral activation of the supplementary motor areas that occurs when we imagine engaging a motor action leads to kinaesthetic feedback from the muscles and builds the basis of the learning mechanism', even though those muscles aren't moving.

Well, I don't know about you but I didn't understand a word of that, so let's look at an example of it at work.

The best example of this that I've found comes from the Cleveland Clinic Foundation in the USA. Researchers there discovered that when fully-awake subjects *imagined* lifting weights with their arms for 15 minutes a day, five days a week for 12 weeks, they actually increased their bicep strength by 13.5 per cent on average and the gain in strength lasted for three months after they stopped the mental exercise regime.[5] If that's what happened during waking visualization, imagine what could be possible in our lucid dreams.

One of the first studies into lucid dream sports training was done way back in 1981, with just six volunteers who, 'after practising complex sports skills that they could do in the waking state already (such as skiing or gymnastics), had the impression that following their lucid dream practice, their sports skills improved.'[6]

This initial study was interesting but inconclusive. Then, in 1990, came a case study that revealed, in bright flashing lights, the potential of lucid dream sports training. An expert in the 'hard forms' of martial arts (tae kwon do/kickboxing) who'd struggled for two years to learn the 'soft forms' (aikido/t'ai chi) managed to transform his practice within just one week by training in lucid dreams. The study describes how, after lucid dream training, he 'amazed his instructor with a nearly perfect defence'.[7]

A couple of decades later, after breakthrough research into lucid dreaming using fMRI technology was released, a new wave of interest developed into lucid dream sports training. Researchers at Heidelberg University in Germany began a series of much larger-scale studies, one involving feedback from over 800 German athletes who were asked about using lucid dreams to practise their athletic disciplines.

This study concluded that 'lucid dreams have a great potential for athletes to use as a training method' because lucid dreaming 'mimics a perfect simulation of the real world' but without the limitations of reality.[8]

I find this one of the most fascinating areas of current lucid dream research – and it makes that extra hour in bed seem far less lazy.

Wanna go deeper?

If you can practise a sport in your lucid dreams, and become a better sportsperson as a result, just think what would happen if you practised kindness and compassion in your lucid dreams? We can train ourselves to be kinder, more loving and more helpful through lucid dreaming, just as we can train ourselves to be better at tennis or martial arts. So whether you choose to be the next Bruce Lee or the next Dalai Lama, you can begin your training in your dreams.

Unpacking our psychological baggage

Lucid dreaming is a free ride into the unconscious mind. However, once we ride into the dream state, we're not freed of our psychological baggage – we often bring that with us. Our fears, habits and prejudices may not be as strong in the lucid dream as they are in the waking state (most people will feel markedly more confident, fearless and joyful once lucid), but they're still definitely there. Amazingly, though, this can offer some very beneficial opportunities to unpack, accept and heal our baggage *within* the dream state.

Scared of spiders? Gradual exposure to spiders within the lucid dream can be used to help overcome a phobia of them in a similar way to cognitive behavioural therapy. By engaging fearlessly with the source of a phobia (whether it's spiders or anything else) within the lucid dream – while holding in mind that it's all a mental projection – sufferers can begin to gradually integrate the phobia.

I've heard from people around the world who've all used their lucid dreams to unpack different aspects of their psychological baggage. One man used his lucid dreams to explore his sexual behaviour – by meeting a dream character who told him he was 'the physical manifestation of your fear of commitment', while a young woman used her lucid dream to meet and forgive the memory of the abuser from her childhood. This potential for healing is one of the deepest benefits of the practice.

Strange but true

Sometimes if the unconscious feels that you're not ready to explore an issue safely, it will simply decline your request to do so. It seems that there's some sort of inherently intelligent self-regulation mechanism within the unconscious that knows just how much we're ready for. I once made a rather audacious request to leave the lucid dream and be taken to heaven. A dream character promptly appeared with a clipboard and said, 'Heaven? You're not ready for that yet.'

You can do it

Two of the biggest bits of baggage connected to our lucid dreaming practice are fear and self-doubt – the fear of what we might find in our unconscious and the self-doubt that makes us think we can't have lucid dreams, or that they are only for special people. This is nonsense! Lucid dreaming is for *everybody* who dreams. If you sleep you dream, and if you dream you can lucid dream – whether you sleep in the park or the palace, lucid dreaming is available to you.

In fact every person reading this has probably had multiple lucid dreams already, even if they don't remember them. This is because children and adolescents naturally lucid dream – not every night and not every child, but the majority of children experience numerous lucid dreams as part of their psychological development.

A 2013 *New Scientist* article wondered whether the 'rewiring of neural circuits during childhood and adolescence may perhaps trigger the heightened brain activity in the frontal regions'[9] that have been linked to lucid awareness. The fact that children and adolescents have spontaneous lucid dreams tells us two important things: firstly that lucid dreaming is a natural, unprompted arising of the human mind (rather than an alien imposition forced upon it), and secondly that you don't need to learn how to lucid dream, you just need to *remember* how.

Think how much easier it is to perform a skill that you learned during childhood, compared to learning it from scratch as an adult – it's the same with remembering how to lucid dream.

Overcoming fear

Some people hold a lot of fear around lucid dreaming – a common yet unnecessary response to the unknown. In my experience it's often the people with the most fear who have the most to gain from the practice – the bigger the dragon the bigger the pot of gold it's guarding.

Once we become lucid, we see ourselves as we really are, warts and all. This can indeed be quite a shock the first time we see it. Once lucid, we may come face to face with everything that we've tried to suppress during our waking hours. Within the Toltec tradition of Mexico, lucid dreaming is an aspect of 'the warrior's path' – this isn't because we do battle with our minds but because it takes the discipline and courage of a warrior to enter into the lucid dream state fearlessly.

As I said before, the dream will only ever present you with what you're ready for, but having said that, I've found that many people are unaware of just how ready they really are.

Another aspect of the fear around lucid dreaming is that we're somehow 'messing with the unconscious'. Rest assured, though: rather than lucidity somehow violating the integrity of the unconscious, it actually allows this integrity to be more fully appreciated. By becoming lucid we're entering into the dream with open arms, not violating it.

Surely it's by *not* remembering, engaging with or working lucidly with our dreams that we truly violate them? Becoming lucid within our dreams is a sign of friendliness, respect and reverence to the sacred space of dreaming. It's a hand of friendship offered to the mystery. Few people see dreams as more sacred or important than lucid dreamers – so embrace lucidity and enter the dream fearlessly!

Self-inception

As lucid dreaming enthusiasts, I'm sure many of you have seen the Hollywood movie *Inception*. This brought lucid dreaming to the masses, and although it got a lot of things wrong (shooting aspects of the unconscious with AK47s, for example) it also got a lot right, including the concept of *incepting* an idea while lucid.

In the movie a group of special agents who can access people's dreams implant, or 'incept', certain suggestions into the dreamers' unconscious minds, in order to alter their actions once they wake up. We can do a similar thing to ourselves – by practising something I call 'self-inception'.

Self-inception is a technique similar to that employed by hypnotherapists, and it can be equally effective. It works by planting the seed of a beneficial idea or suggestion into the fertile soil of our unconscious while lucid dreaming. When we become lucid the seed penetrates the deepest levels of the mind and can affect our waking state in a profound way. Within Tibetan Buddhism it's believed that 'the mind is up to seven times more powerful'[10] in the lucid dream state, so it's no surprise that self-inception works so well.

So how do we actually do it? By going into the lucid dream state and calling out beneficial suggestions or statements of intent. In doing this, we can implant a new habit pattern in our minds. For example, if you've been struggling with self-worth, once lucid you could call out: 'I am loved, loving and loveable in every single way, I am loved, loving and loveable every single day.' This is a particularly powerful affirmation to use while dreaming or awake actually.

Self-inception works with addictive behaviour too. In the same way that a hypnotherapist implants a beneficial suggestion pertaining to altering an addictive behaviour pattern, a lucid dreamer might implant a beneficial suggestion once lucid.

Alternatively, it's possible to go straight to the source of the problem, as the subject of our first case study discovered. Antonio had been struggling with his addiction to cigarettes for more than 10 years until one night, while in a lucid dream, he decided to ask his brain to help him quit. What happened next is astonishing.

Case study: Conquering nicotine addiction

Dreamer: *Antonio, UK*

Age: *37*

The lowdown from Antonio: *'I'd been smoking for about 10 years before it happened. I'd listened to Charlie's talk in the chill-out tent at the Secret Garden Party festival and it inspired me to try and work with my addiction. Oh, and I just want to clarify that I was completely sober that weekend (I'm not a huge drinker and I'm not really into anything else either), but I was smoking, as usual. The cigarettes I had that night turned out to be the last ones I'd ever smoke, though.'*

Antonio's dream report: *'I was in the middle of a dream in which I was running around a castle. There were other characters there, some running with me, others running away. I caught a reflection of myself and noticed a kind of blue glue coming off my face and* body and I thought, That's peculiar. *I then asked myself,* Am I dreaming? *and looked at the palm of my hand, as Charlie had suggested. I saw the blue glue covering it, and realized I was dreaming!*

'At this point I became terribly excited, but I remembered to remain calm to avoid waking up. I said to myself, Okay, breathe, calm down. *Then I noticed that one of the characters who was running with me, a young woman, was looking at me calmly. And then began the conversation.'*

Me: 'Am I dreaming?'

The woman: 'Yes.'

Me: 'So who are you?'

The woman: 'I'm your brain.'

Me: 'What? You're my brain!?'

The woman: 'Yes. What would you like to do?'

Me: 'Er, can I ask you a question?'

The woman: 'Sure.'

Me: 'I worry about my health and I want to know if everything's okay.'

The woman: 'You're fine, in perfect health. But do us all a favour and stop smoking. It bothers us.'

Me: 'Yeah. Well... Okay then. How about whenever I feel like a cigarette you make me think or do something else instead?'

The woman: 'Sure, that's easy.'

'Then suddenly I wake up in my tent. I wake my boyfriend, who's next to me, and say, "I just had a lucid dream." He replies, "Tell the guys," and suddenly I'm not in my tent but in a car and there are some people in the back seat. I realize I'm still dreaming! I'm having a false awakening! Then I actually wake up for real, in my tent at the festival.'

Life since the dream: *'I know it's hard to believe but since that dream I haven't smoked at all and it's been almost six months now. I'm quite happy and impressed by the power of it. It seems like the effect of the dream lasted long enough for the addiction to pass. I've even been around smokers and have had no desire to smoke. I've also travelled a lot and not felt like smoking while waiting at airports as I always used to. I still can't quite believe it.*

'Oh yeah, and a few weeks ago, when my boyfriend asked me to buy some stuff for him at the supermarket, I bought everything on the list but completely forgot the cigarettes! I guess my brain made me think of something else. Weird, eh?'

This case study is particularly fascinating for two reasons. Firstly, Antonio had done hardly anything to bring on this lucid dream, apart from listening to a 45-minute talk that I'd given at a music festival the day before. Secondly, the results of the healing were spectacular: 10 years of nicotine addiction cured in one lucid dream! At the time of going to press, it has been more than 18 months since he last smoked.

Antonio managed to get into that lucid dream without much effort, other than a very good reason, i.e. to quit smoking, and a very helpful unconscious mind, but many people, myself included, need to know the tools of the trade before we can have lucid dreams on a regular basis. So, let's open our second toolbox of lucid dreaming techniques and make that happen.

TOOLBOX 2: GETTING TO KNOW THE TERRITORY

As every explorer knows, before you set off on an adventure it's vital to be aware of the territory. So, in order to become lucid in our dreams, we need to get to know the territory of our dreams.

My meditation teacher and mentor is a Zimbabwean-born mindfulness meditation expert called Rob Nairn. Rob spent much of his youth exploring the southern African bush, and one day he told me about the concept of 'bush eyes'. Apparently, people who've spent a lot of time walking through the bush develop a capacity to see it more clearly, with a broad, panoramic vision that means they hardly ever step on snakes or trip over logs. Their eyes have become so attuned to the terrain that they see clearly as they move through it. They've acquired 'bush eyes'.

In a similar way, people who've spent a lot of time working with their dreams often develop a sort of 'dream eyes' in which they know the territory of their dream world so well that they too avoid stepping on snakes or tripping over logs, so to speak.

Dream work is a process of reorientation in which we explore the territory of our dream world through a new perspective of enquiry and understanding. One of the key aspects of our dreams, which we need to enquire into and try to understand, is dream signs.

Dream signs

If I blindfolded you and took you into a bakery, I reckon you'd still be able to tell me where you were, right? Although you couldn't see the bakery, its smells, sounds and atmosphere would be enough to indicate your whereabouts. You've smelled the aromas of a bakery and experienced its atmosphere so many times that you're able to recognize one even through a blindfold.

In the same way, we can come to recognize the dream state, even when blindfolded by non-lucidity. How? By getting to know its unique sights, sounds and atmosphere. This forms the basis of spotting dream signs.

A dream sign is any improbable, impossible or bizarre aspect of dream experience that can indicate we're dreaming. Most people's dreams are full of dream signs – things as far out as talking dogs and dead relatives or as subtle as dreaming of being back at school. Basically, if it's something that doesn't usually occur in waking life, it may well be a dream sign.

There are many different categories of dream sign, but I classify them into three main groups:

❖ Anomalous: random, one-off anomalies such as talking fish or ninja babies.

❖ Thematic: dreamlike themes or scenarios such as being back at school or being naked in public.

❖ Recurring: dream signs that have appeared multiple times. These are a real boon for lucid dreamers.

One of the most important reasons for keeping a dream diary (see toolbox 1) is to record and chart our personal dream signs. But how does all this lead to lucid dreams? By acknowledging our particular dream signs in the waking state we create a lucidity *trigger* that'll be activated the next time we see that dream sign, thus triggering lucidity.

Five steps to spotting dream signs

1. Once you've recalled and written down your dreams, read back through them, on the lookout for dream signs.

2. If you dreamed that you were walking down a street and saw Barack Obama standing next to a blue dragon, then your dream signs would be 'Barack Obama' and 'blue dragon'. Unless you're Hillary Clinton, of course, in which case seeing Barack Obama wouldn't be a dream sign because he's a feature of your everyday life. The blue dragon, however, would still be a dream sign.

3. If you've dreamed of a blue dragon several times, this would be a recurring dream sign. Recurring dream signs mean recurring opportunities to become lucid!

4. Once you've pinpointed your dream signs, make a determined effort to be on the lookout for them in future. This effort will permeate your dreams, and eventually you'll start recognizing dream signs while you're dreaming and become lucid.

5. Before bed, remind yourself again and again: *The next time I see Barack Obama* (or whatever your particular dream signs are), *I'll know that I'm dreaming!* Then, when you next dream about your dream sign, the lucidity trigger will be activated, making you spontaneously think, *Barack Obama? Aha! This is a dream sign, I must be dreaming!*

Once you've discovered your dream signs, set a strong intention to recognize them the next time they show up in your dreams. One classic dream sign is of course a talking frog, like the one in the following story.

The frog from the well

There once was a frog who lived in a well. This frog had never left his well, and to him it was his entire world. Then one day a frog from the ocean hopped into the well and after exchanging pleasantries the frog from the well asked the frog from the ocean a question:

'So, where do you live, then?'

The frog from the ocean replied, 'I live in the ocean.'

'The ocean, eh? What's that?'

The frog from the ocean considered the question before replying: 'The ocean is a bit like your well but much, much bigger.'

The frog from the well couldn't believe that anything could be bigger than his well. 'Bigger than my well? Impossible! Your ocean is probably about a quarter of the size of my well.'

'No, no, the ocean is much bigger than your well!' protested the frog from the ocean.

'Okay then, about half the size?'

'No way! It's the ocean – it's huge, it's vast, it's immeasurable!'

'It's really that big, is it? Okay then, let's agree that your ocean must be about the same size as my well?'

In despair the frog from the ocean said, 'Look, why don't you come and see the ocean for yourself?'

With indignant confidence the frog from the well replied, 'Okay then, let's go!'

And so they both hopped out of the well and down a path that the frog from the well had never dared go. At the end of the path the view opened up to reveal the huge panorama of the nearby ocean. The frog from the ocean smiled and said: 'See, much bigger than your well!'

The frog from the well looked in awe at the vastness of the ocean and then his head exploded into a thousand pieces. The end.

You're probably wondering what the hell this weird story about surprisingly well-mannered frogs with exploding heads has to do with lucid dreaming, right? It's like this: most of us view our dreams like the frog from the well viewed his world – limited, subjective and hugely underestimated. But in fact our dreams can be oceanic experiences of transpersonal insight and clarity that'll make our limitations (rather than our heads) explode into a thousand pieces.

So how can we learn to 'see beyond the well'? The first step is to believe that it's possible. The next step is actively to request access to these deeper parts of our mind. By actively asking for dreams that let us see beyond the 'well of our own experience' we may start to begin dreaming in a far less limited way.

The guided meditation exercise below is designed to help us extend the hand of friendship to our unconscious, asking it to show us its oceanic depths and in turn to offer us dream signs, insights and opportunities to become lucid.

Seeing beyond the well

This is an exercise in which we ask to 'see beyond the well' but before we do that we express gratitude – first to our body, then to our mind and then to our inner 'dreamer' and the amazing dreams that it creates. This meditation can be done first in the daytime and then (once you can remember all the steps) in the hypnagogic state before sleep. You might also like to listen to a recording of it.

Step 1

❖ Find a relaxed position, either sitting upright with a straight back, or lying down.

❖ Breathe through the nose or mouth, either is fine, and come into an awareness of the breath.

❖ Drop any notions of stopping your thoughts or of emptying the mind. Simply breathe and follow the guidance of this meditation. Let thoughts come and go naturally, simply knowing when you're breathing in and when you're breathing out.

❖ After a few minutes, move your focus from your breath to your body. Become aware of your body as it sits or lies in space. Allow yourself to open up to a feeling of gratitude towards your body.

Step 2

- ❖ I invite you to bring your attention first to your legs. Really *feel* your legs and take a moment to consider and acknowledge the amazing job they do. Your legs are amazing! But have you ever said 'thank you' to your legs?

- ❖ Take a moment now – in your own way, in your own mind – to show gratitude to your legs. Say 'thank you' to your legs, now.

- ❖ Next, bring your awareness to your arms and hands. These limbs that allow you to write, to eat, to touch, to hug. Your arms and hands are amazing! Take a moment to show gratitude to them for the brilliant job that they do. Say 'thank you' to your arms and hands, now.

- ❖ Next, bring your entire body into your awareness and into your gratitude. Be aware of your entire body as it sits or lies in space. Be aware of your feet, legs, core, chest, hands, arms, head and neck. Be aware of your digestive system, your nervous system, your ever beating heart.

- ❖ What a miracle your body is – it's remarkable. Always working hard and always trying its best. However ill or broken it may seem, your body is always trying its best and so let's show gratitude for that. Take a moment to say 'thank you' to your entire body, now.

- ❖ Next, bring your awareness from the physical to the mental. Bring your awareness to your mind and show gratitude for its creativity and genius. Say 'thank you' to your mind now.

- ❖ Finally, bring your awareness to your inner dreamer, the part of your unconscious mind that creates and plays out your dreams. Give thanks to the dreamer; give thanks for the dreams. Say 'thank you' to your inner dreamer, now.

Step 3

❖ By showing gratitude to your body, your mind and your inner dreamer you've opened up a direct line of communication to the deepest depths of yourself, and it's to this deepest part that you now make your request.

❖ Ask to see 'see beyond the well'. Just as the frog from the well did, ask to move beyond your limitations and to have dreams that allow you to see the oceanic vastness of your own potential. Ask your inner dreamer to let you 'see beyond the well', now.

❖ The dreamer is part of you; the dreams it creates are part of your mind so ask for what you want to find, and ask for what you want your dreams to show you. Ask for dreams of insight, ask for lucid dreams, ask to see the ocean of your own potential. Make your request now.

❖ One final time, ask your dreamer, in your own words, in your own way, to let you see beyond the well now.

❖ And to conclude, take a moment to dedicate the beneficial energy of this meditation to all beings.

After undertaking this meditation exercise be sure to write down any and all of your dreams – the night that follows especially, and the next one, too – because you've just made a very powerful request to your inner dreamer and you may find that your dreams become very big, very soon.

A road map of sleep

In the same way that the territory of a country is divided into sections on a map, the territory of our sleep is mapped out into various sections too. If we want to dream lucidly then we need to understand *when* we're most likely to be dreaming, so we can schedule our lucid dreaming practice accordingly.

With this in mind, let's take a moment to learn about the land in which we spend a third of our lives. These days, most sleep scientists break sleep up into four sections or stages.[11]

Stage 1: Hypnagogic

This is the first stage of sleep: the hypnagogic state. It's very light sleep, experienced by many as more of a heavy drowsiness than sleep, and it's often accompanied by alpha brain wave patterns of relaxed wakefulness. The most recognizable aspect of stage 1 sleep is the hypnagogic imagery: the dreamy hallucinations that flash and fade before our mind's eye as we drift off.

Stage 2: Light, dreamless sleep

Most people experience this as a light but dreamless sleep. We've now moved from the semi-conscious hypnagogic into the blackout stage of sleep, but we are yet to start dreaming.

Stage 3: Deep sleep

We now fall much further into sleep as our brain begins producing delta brain waves and we enter into the deepest level of dreamless sleep. Stage 3 is restorative sleep. It's the state in which we release HGH (human growth hormone), repair our cells and recharge the batteries. If you manage to wake somebody from the deep, delta-wave blackout of Stage 3, they'll commonly feel groggy and disorientated.

Rapid eye movement (REM)

This is the stage where our body becomes paralysed, our brain becomes highly active and we dream. Although some dream imagery can occasionally seep into all stages of sleep it's REM in which we dream most abundantly.

Most people have about four or five 90-minute sleep cycles per night, with REM dreaming being a feature of every one of these. That's about four or five dream periods a night, which become almost 1,800 dreams per year and well over 100,000 dreams in a lifetime. That's 100,000 opportunities to get lucid!

The journey into sleep

We don't just *fall* asleep. Sleep is a cyclical journey, from waking-state drowsiness to the depths of deep sleep and then up into the realm of dreaming.

Let's take a look at our sleep road map. When we first fall asleep, the initial progression from stage 1 to stage 3 takes about half an hour or so. After hanging out in deep sleep for another 30 minutes or so, we travel briefly back up into stage 2, but then, rather than continuing back to stage 1 hypnagogic, we enter REM and begin to dream.

Our eyes display rapid movements (REM), our body becomes paralysed and we experience the succession of imagery, narrative and emotional experience that we call dreaming. As we learned earlier, dreaming is an active sleep state – we're not resting while we dream.

Our first dream period is only about 10 minutes long, and so the whole cycle, from the hypnagogic state to the end of our first REM period, usually takes about 90 minutes. We repeat this 90-minute cycle multiple times throughout the night, but with each cycle we spend increasingly more time in REM and less time in deep sleep. As our REM periods get longer, the last two hours of our sleep end up consisting almost entirely of dreaming.

The last few hours of our sleep cycle are also when we'll enter dreams most easily from the waking state. This makes it prime time for lucid dreaming. While you can have lucid dreams in the first few hours of your sleep cycle, the dream periods will be short and your mind may be quite groggy. However, in the last few hours you'll not only have longer dream periods but also a fair few hours of sleep under your belt, so your mind will feel fresh and ready to engage lucidity.

When you wake up (at any point in your sleep cycle) you always pass through a state called the hypnopompic. This much-overlooked state of consciousness is the gateway from sleep to waking, and, if we can harness it, holds some of the highest rewards. In toolbox 6 we'll touch on how to use the full potential of the hypnopompic.

Although the majority of people may sleep in the way described above, you may not be part of that majority, so get to know how *you* sleep, not how everybody else does.

Remember: the first half of the night is mainly deep sleep with short dream periods and the second half is mainly dreaming with not much entry into deep sleep.

The hypnagogic state

One of the most accessible parts of the journey into sleep is found in the hypnagogic – the transitional state of mind that lies between wakefulness and sleep. It's the drowsy, in-between stage often characterized by the hypnagogic imagery – the visual or sometimes conceptual displays that we experience as we drift off to sleep.

These hypnagogic hallucinations are made up of memories of the day, mental preoccupations and displays of the mind's content. For most people the hypnagogic state can seem as mad as a bag of badgers, but if befriended it can be harnessed to tap into a deeply creative source.

We pass through the hypnagogic state every time we fall asleep, which means we have a daily opportunity to engage it with awareness. As is indicated by the word 'hypnagogic', this is a state not dissimilar to the hypnotic trance state, and in fact my hypnosis teacher, the late Mervyn Minall-Jones, once told me (in his broad Australian accent): 'Charlie mate, you enter a state of hypnosis twice a day! When you fall asleep through the hypnagogic and when you wake up through the hypnopompic.'

As we enter the hypnagogic state we might experience sudden spasms known as 'myoclonic jerks'. Some researchers believe that this is an evolutionary throwback to when we used to sleep in trees – the jerk would help us maintain awareness of our sleeping space so we didn't fall out of the tree.

Most often people just zonk out and 'fall' asleep but if we really want to get to know the territory of the hypnagogic we need to *float* rather than fall. The hypnagogic is a state of huge potential, but how can we spend more time in it than the 10 or so minutes that it usually takes us to fall asleep? We must learn simply to hang out in it.

Five steps to hanging out in the hypnagogic

The aim of this practice is to stay in the hypnagogic mindfully without entering into the sleep that lies beyond it. This is a practice from the Mindfulness of Dream and Sleep approach rather than a lucid dreaming technique per se, but my advice is this: get to know your hypnagogic state well because it's the gateway into the dream. The best way to extend our experience of the hypnagogic is to enter it during the daytime. Here's how:

1. At a time when you're drowsy but not too tired, find a place where you can lie down. On top of the bed is fine, but not *in* it. We don't want to fall asleep, remember.

2. Set an alarm for 20 minutes later (just in case you fall asleep) and then simply lie down on your back with a pillow under your head and close your eyes.

3. In the afternoon hours most people will enter into the hypnagogic within about five to 15 minutes. Once you're in the hypnagogic aim to stay there for about 10 minutes if you can. Just rest in it, watching the imagery and being aware of the waves of drowsy energy that wash through it. Maintaining awareness of your breathing and of your bodily sensations will help keep you from falling asleep.

4. After 20 minutes your alarm will sound, so gently bring yourself back to fully wakeful awareness.

5. Alternatively, you could just go to bed half an hour earlier, allowing yourself to intentionally float into sleep more slowly than usual. Find what works for you and enjoy it.

If you like the sound of this practice then you might want to check out my CD of guided sleep mediations – *Lucid Dreaming, Conscious Sleeping* – which contains a 25-minute guided hypnagogic meditation. It's available to buy or download online.

CHARLIE'S TOOLBOX CHECKLIST

❖ Get to know the territory of your sleep and dreams. Remember, the aim is for bush eyes!

❖ There are three types of dream sign: anomalous, thematic and recurring. Record them all but pay particular attention to the recurring ones.

❖ Ask to 'see beyond the well' and allow your limitations to explode, just like the frog's head!

❖ There are four stages of sleep – hypnagogic, light sleep, deep sleep and REM dreaming. Your REM periods increase as the night progresses so focus your attention on the last few hours of your sleep cycle.

❖ Learn to hang out in the hypnagogic state. Many of the techniques that we'll explore later are based on an ability to maintain your awareness in the hypnagogic, so it's well worth the practice.

❖ Don't forget to keep up the dream diary!

Chapter 3
The three pillars, career paths and creativity

Now that you're beginning to 'see beyond the well', dream deeply and spot your dream signs, you're probably becoming aware of just how bizarre your dream world can be. The most important thing to remember is that whatever comes up in your dreams is totally okay, and that whatever dream content you bear witness to is fine, just as it is.

Scary dreams, sexy dreams and violent dreams are all simply expressions of the dreaming mind and should not be judged on the basis of our waking-state sensibilities. This attitude of non-judgemental openness forms the basis of the way I teach lucid dreaming at my workshops, and also of my 'three pillars' approach.

The three pillars of lucidity

I've taught thousands of people lucid dreaming, and through observing them I've come to realize there are three main qualities that lead to a balanced, beneficial and fruitful lucid dreaming practice. Engagement of these qualities is what separates the tourists from the travellers: those who lucid dream just for the scenery and those who do it to discover new realms of possibility. These qualities are acceptance, friendliness and kindness: the three pillars of lucidity practice.

Acceptance

Once we become aware of our dreams we need to accept that everything we're experiencing, or at least 99 per cent of it, is part of our own mind. However disturbed, violent or dark the contents of the dream may seem, we must try to understand that it's just part of our own oceanic psyche and simply wants to be seen. The unconscious mind wants us to bear witness to it, but to do that we have to drop the notion that the dream is somehow separate from us.

When people find something 'bad' or unpleasant in their dreams, lucid or otherwise, they often think that it's their duty to try and change it, or 'put it right'. This is unwise and unnecessary, because simply by bearing witness to these disowned aspects of our unconscious we allow repressed parts of our psyche to become integrated naturally. It's just as the great Indian spiritual teacher Krishnamurti once said, 'The seeing is the doing.' But this is dependent upon accepting whatever is *seen* to be part of us.

I spoke to mindfulness expert Rob Nairn about this recently, and he told me that 'the conditions for change are created instantaneously by acceptance, whereas non-acceptance creates internal struggle and psychological conflict because we're literally fighting our Self'. He added that 'the psychological force of seeing is all we need to do to have insights. We need do nothing more than bear witness to the mind's display with acceptance.'[1]

It's important to say that the use of the word 'acceptance' here doesn't mean the approval or endorsement of negative mind states or situations. Acceptance is a quality of mind that is a prerequisite to engaging compassionately a situation and being able to work with it.

I've met some dreamers who believe that dark external forces are entering their lucid dreams when in fact they're simply meeting their own 'shadow' – an amazing opportunity for lucid dream integration so often lost through a basic lack of acceptance. We'll explore shadow integration fully in the next chapter.

Friendliness

Once we accept that 99% of everything we're experiencing in the lucid dream is part of our own psyche, we can then engage the second pillar of our practice: friendliness. This means unconditional friendliness towards all situations within the dream, good and bad. Friendliness towards ourselves, friendliness towards the dream characters, towards seemingly 'negative' manifestations and positive ones. Having an attitude of friendliness will open up a whole vista of the dream once hidden from view.

The Tibetan Buddhist master Mingyur Rinpoche says: 'If you reject a negative mental emotion it will become your enemy, but if you indulge it then it becomes the boss of you. So what do we do with a negative emotion? What's the best method? Face it, make friends with it!' So it is with our lucid dreams. If we accept that almost everything in the dream is us, then why would we ever *not* be friendly to it?

Kindness

And finally, the third pillar of a stable lucid dreaming practice is kindness. Be kind to everything in the lucid dream, for it's all you. Well, 99 per cent of it is you. And what about that crucial 1 per cent that might be something other than your own mind? More about that later, but until then, be kind to that too. As the Dalai Lama famously said: 'Be kind wherever possible. It is always possible.'

By cultivating these three mental attitudes of acceptance, friendliness and kindness as part of our lucid dream training, they become three pillars, holding up the entire structure of our lucid dream practice and providing shelter from the winds of dualistic superstition that so often blow through our waking mind.

Creative dreaming

Another aspect of mind that many people are unwilling to accept as theirs is that of their inner creative genius. Through lucid dreaming we can get to know this genius on its home turf.

The lucid dream state is a great place to get creative, as it offers us 'direct contact to the remarkable creative reserves of the human mind'.[2] But how does this work? Well, our dreams are powered almost exclusively by the right hemisphere of the brain, which specializes in creativity, imagination and non-linear thought processing. Neurologists tell us that the right hemisphere is 'by its design, spontaneous and imaginative... [a place in which] our artistic juices flow freely without inhibition or judgement'.[3]

Often, however, our lack of awareness in dreams means that we miss out on the creative potential that our dreaming mind offers. If only we could tap into that creative genius in real time. Once we become lucid though, we can. Lucidity brings a strand of left-brain cognizance into the dream, meaning that we can intentionally engage the dream's right- brain creativity.

All this makes the lucid dream state the perfect place for reflecting on life choices and asking for creative advice from the unconscious mind. From a Tibetan Buddhist point of view once we're lucid we're actually closer to our fully enlightened nature than while we're awake, meaning that any creative endeavours we engage in while lucid might offer a depth of perspective unmatched by waking-state rumination. For more information about tapping into the enlightened potential of the lucid dreaming mind, check out my first book *Dreams of Awakening*.

The unconscious mind sees much more than we do, and so it has much larger resources of knowledge from which to offer solutions to our daily life challenges. What career path should I take? How can I be of most benefit to those around me? How would that character in my new book feel in this situation? These are just some of the creative questions we can explore within the infinite originality of the lucid dream state.

One woman who knows more about creative lucid dreaming than most is British author Dr Clare Johnson, who wrote a PhD on the link between lucid dreaming and the creative process. Clare used her lucid dreams to take on the personas of characters in the novel she was writing – as a way to experience their thoughts and feelings.

She has also asked her unconscious mind to help with plot revisions in her books, and has even used the lucid dream state to win the famous 'Dream Telepathy Contest' at the International Association of the Study of Dreams annual congress. Let's hear some of her top tips for dream creativity.

Tips from the pros: Creative lucidity, with Dr Clare Johnson

Watch your dream film
A balance between the unconscious and the conscious is recognized as the brain state where creative thinking happens, whether we're awake or asleep. In a lucid dream you can consciously experience the mesmeric cinema of your unconscious at play, so simply watching your 'dream film' and seeing how it responds to your thoughts and emotions is a stimulating artistic resource. You can bring weird and wonderful images, plotlines and adventures back to the waking state and turn them into art and stories.

Be a dream magician!
Nudging the lucid dream can trigger a specific creative reaction. Decide to find a magic box full of ideas or 'things never created before', ask the dream for help with a project, or walk into an art gallery intending to see a painting you love and then memorize every detail until you wake up. Expectation and intent are powerful forces in lucid dreaming: if lucidity is stable and you fully expect to receive creative inspiration, you will.

Shrug off your inner critic

In lucid dreams it's easy to do this as you're in the wild, original world of the unconscious where the critical self has much less of a voice. So draw on the natural creativity of lucid dreaming to perfect your snowboarding in a replica of the waking world, or practise a new art form.

Try glass-blowing, sculpting, singing in the voice of an opera singer or swooping and twirling through a dance sequence. There are no limits! Lucid dreaming can expand your life experience and give you the confidence to experiment with new art forms in waking life.

Connect with your inner Einstein

Associative thinking and creative problem-solving can reach great heights in lucid dreams. Ask the dream directly for help and you may find a voice booms an answer, or you'll be shown a scene or an image that answers your question. If nothing happens, open a door and expect to find the answer behind it. Lucid dreamers have received creative help in everything from computer programming and video-game design to health issues and relationships.

Practise a waking version of lucid dreaming

Here's my Lucid Writing Technique: close your eyes, bring your attention to your breath, and relax into a light trance. Then focus on a lucid dream image and allow it to move and transform in your mind's eye. You can guide this mental imagery if you want, or just see what happens.

When you feel ready, open your eyes slightly, just enough to be able to write down what you see. Write as fast as you can, without thinking critically. Let the writing go wherever it wants to go. Lucid Writing can trigger new ideas, dissolve artistic blocks and resolve nightmares, and it's a fun way of exploring the creative energy of lucid dreams.

Dr Clare Johnson's novels, *Breathing in Colour* and *Dreamrunner*, are both lucid dream-inspired. Visit www.clarejay.com for more information about her work.

Strange but true

The Scottish author Robert Louis Stevenson had a novel approach to dealing with writer's block. He would ask specifically for a dream containing the essence of his next story. On one such occasion he dreamed a dream that would provide the basis of his famous *Dr Jekyll and Mr Hyde*.[4]

Trust in the dream

The enlightened knowledge that we all possess can often seem quite inaccessible in the waking state, but through lucid dreaming we can reach it much more easily, and perhaps even access the transpersonal collective wisdom which lies beyond the dream.

It seems that, in a lucid dream, when we ask a dream character a question we're asking it of the tiny aspect of our psyche that particular dream character represents. This means that the answer we get will be inherently limited. But if we ask the dream *itself* (by calling the question out to the sky or any other open space in the dream) then the answer may be sourced from a far broader and more powerful aspect of our dreaming mind.

I encourage you to trust the wisdom of your own unconscious. Not blindly, of course – for we need to be sure that we don't interpret the often symbolic language of the unconscious too literally – but we can still learn to heed its advice because once we're lucid it's not 'just a dream', it's communication with our inner wisdom.

So, if there's a certain issue or non-beneficial mind pattern that's holding you back in your waking state, you can choose to explore creatively that issue within the safety of your own dream. You can even go into the lucid dream state and make a request such as, 'What shall I do with my career?', as the subject of our next case study did, with life-changing results.

Case study: Choosing a new career path

Dreamer: *Nina, UK*

Age: *29*

The lowdown from Nina: *'I was really stuck for what to do, career-wise. I felt as if I was just stagnating in my job as a dance teacher – although I enjoyed it, I felt it wasn't really challenging me every day. I'd had quite a few dreams in which I'd become lucid and would ask the dream, "What shall I do with my career?" Often nothing would really happen, but I stuck with it and after the third time of asking I got a really big answer.'*

Nina's dream report: *'I was dreaming that I was in my bedroom. I looked out of the window, saw that it looked different and then I became lucid. I flew out of the window and asked the dream, "What should I do, career-wise?" Then I floated down the building and looked through the window into a room. In there, I could see a very clear image of me sitting on the floor, surrounded by books and reading to young children.*

Then I woke up. I felt a bit confused as to what the lucid dream signified, but I took it to mean I should work with children.

'In light of that dream, I started to apply for various roles working with children, but I didn't get anywhere with it. Then, a few weeks later, I randomly saw a teaching role come up in a primary school near my home. It wasn't with the kind of youngsters that I'd seen in the dream, but it was still a job working with children, so I applied for it.

'The night before the interview, I had another lucid dream. Once lucid I called out to the dream: "Shall I do this job?" Suddenly, in the sky above me, the stars rearranged themselves into a constellation that clearly spelled out the word "yes". I then called out to the dream, "Can you help me to get the job please?", to which the stars rearranged again to form the words "Yes, millions." It was amazing! And then I woke up.'

Life since the dream: *'The next day I went to the interview and was told that the job I had applied for was already taken but one with young children had just become available. I applied for that one instead and ended up getting the job. I love my new role and it all makes sense now. I spend my days sitting on the floor surrounded by books and reading to young children, just as I'd seen myself doing in my lucid dream.'*

When Nina emailed me this dream, I was moved to tears. Not only was it such a powerful example of how the unconscious often sees much further and much more clearly than our conscious mind does, but it also resonated with a dream of my own in which I, too, asked my unconscious what I should do with my life. It told me to trust in myself, take a leap of faith and have the confidence to follow my passion for lucid dreaming. I did just that. Lucid dreaming really can make your dreams come true.

So, now that we're beginning to see just how life-changing and creative lucid dreams can be, this seems like a great time to get back to the toolshed and learn some of the most powerful techniques for inducing them: reality checks, the Weird technique and the Columbo method!

TOOLBOX 3: LOOKING CLOSELY

Becoming lucid in our dreams is a training based primarily on recognition: recognizing that what we thought was real-life is in fact a dream. As part of our training in recognition we need to start *looking closely* in both our dream and waking lives...

This next section is where some of you might think I'm one spanner short of a toolbox. Then I give you the full explanation and you think I'm a little less crazy, but still crazy. Then you have a dream in which you experience what I'm about to tell you, and you email me at 4 a.m. saying: 'You're *not* crazy! I saw my hand change!' Let me explain...

Reality checks

One of the most common entries into a lucid dream is simply spotting a dream sign and becoming lucid. But sometimes, even though you've spotted a dream sign and are sure that you must be dreaming, the rest of the dream looks so realistic that you simply can't accept that you're in a dream. This is when you need something called reality checks.

Dr Stephen LaBerge and the researchers at the Lucidity Institute in California have scientifically verified that there are certain things that are virtually impossible for the human mind to replicate consistently within the pre-lucid dream state (the state just before you're lucid), and so these can be used to confirm reliably whether or not you're dreaming. Reality checks will almost always be performed in the pre-lucid dream state, because if you're conscious enough to think, *I should do a reality check*, then you're often almost lucid already.

There are lots of different reality checks, but I'll take you through some of my favourites:

- ✦ Looking at your outstretched hand twice in quick succession without it changing in some way.

- ✦ Reading text coherently twice without it changing in some way.

- ✦ Using digital or electrical devices without them changing or malfunctioning in some way.

During a dream, the brain is working flat out to maintain the projection of our elaborately detailed dreamscape in real time, and although it's amazingly good at this, once pre-lucid it often struggles to replicate the detail of an intricate image (such as a piece of text or an outstretched hand) twice in quick succession. So, if we try to make it engage in such a replication, it will provide a close but imperfect rendering, and it's the acknowledgement of this imperfect rendering that makes us lucidly aware.

Take a reality check

Let's explore those three reality checks in more depth:

Looking at your hands

If you think you might be dreaming, but you're not 100 per cent sure, look at your outstretched hand *within* the dream, then quickly look away and look back at it again. Alternatively, watch your hand as you flip it over and back again. Either way, your brain will usually struggle to reproduce an identical projection of your hand, so on second glance it may be a strange shape, perhaps missing a finger or two, or look dappled or transformed.

When you look at your hand twice in a row the dreaming brain tries its best to reproduce exactly the same image, but it doesn't quite have the processing speed to do so perfectly. The variations are multiple, but the result is singular: if you really *expect* your hand to change, it *will* change.

I know the hand-checking thing can sometimes be a bit hard to imagine, so let me break it down for you:

❖ You're in a dream, something weird happens and you think you might be dreaming. You look at your hand, flip it over (with the expectation that it'll change if you're dreaming) and when you flip it back, it probably will have changed in some way.

❖ The dreaming mind is very creative (I've seen my hand turn into a baby elephant and grow three new fingers!), but it's not very good at replicating precise detail. Hands are pretty detailed, so it really struggles to replicate them to order.

Reading text

Within a pre-lucid dream it's virtually impossible to read any text coherently twice in succession. LaBerge's research laboratory found that in lucid dreams text changed 75 per cent of the time as the dreamer was reading it and 95 per cent of the time on second reading.[5]

So, you're in a dream and you think you might be dreaming, try to read something. The text will often be unintelligible, move around as you're reading it, or in some cases just fade away altogether. All these are signs that you're dreaming.

Using digital or electrical appliances

Just as the mind struggles to reproduce text, so it also struggles with the highly detailed screen of a smartphone or a computer, which will often seem blurred and transformed in a pre-lucid dream as the dreaming mind struggles to project it accurately.

I know it sounds crazy, but it's often impossible to read a digital watch, successfully operate any form of digital or electrical appliance or switch a light on and off. This works on the principle that if you flick a light switch within a dream you're asking the dreaming mind to project an exact replication of the dreamscape but in a totally different light and shadow setting, literally at the flick of a switch. This is something that it finds almost impossible to do.

Remember: If you think you might be dreaming but want to be 100 per cent sure (before you try to fly through the sky) look at anything with a detailed pattern – such as your hand – twice in a row and if it changes you'll know for sure that you're definitely dreaming.

Although opportunities for reality checks will often crop up in your dreams naturally, they're usually only engaged once you spot a dream sign and need confirmation of your present reality. You can, however, actively hasten the process by getting into the habit of conducting reality checks while you're *awake*. This is the basis of the Weird technique – a deceptively simple method through which I have the majority of my lucid dreams. Here's how to do it:

The Weird technique

❖ As you go about your daily life, whenever something weird happens, or whenever you experience synchronicity, déjà vu, a strange coincidence or any other type of dreamlike anomaly, ask yourself,

'Am I dreaming?' and then answer this question by doing a reality check.

❖ By doing reality checks during the daytime (whenever something weird happens) this new habit will soon reappear in your dreams. But when you check your hand in your dream it will change and you'll become lucid!

❖ If you spend your day packing boxes what might you dream about that night? Packing boxes, right? And so by spending your day asking yourself, 'Am I dreaming?' and then doing a reality check, that night you may well dream about doing that too. But when you dream about doing it, the reality check will indicate that you're dreaming and lead to lucidity.

Okay, wait, what do I do again?

Whenever you see something weird or unexpected in your daily life take a moment to think, *That's weird, could I be dreaming right now?* Then perform a reality check and, as long as your hand doesn't grow an extra finger or morph into a baby elephant, you can be sure that you're definitely not dreaming. This sets up a habit that'll crop up in your dreams too, but in your dreams the hand *will* change and you *will* become lucid.

Let me elucidate further with an amusing example. A rather weird-looking friend of mine, a Buddhist monk, was at an interfaith conference recently and a young lucid dreamer took one look at him (in his *weird* robes, with his *weird* shaved head, and his *weird* inner calm) and then did a reality check by looking at his hand, flipping it over and back again.

My monk friend – who knows all about lucid dreaming and the Weird technique – thought to himself, *That's weird, I've just been reality checked* and then proceeded to do a similar reality check to make sure that *he* wasn't dreaming! Weird, eh?

> **Strange but true**
>
> Lucid dreaming specialist Daniel Love has calculated that '11 per cent of our mental experience each day is spent dreaming'. He says, 'Just to clarify, this is not 11 per cent of sleeping activity but 11 per cent of your entire daily experience each and every day.'[6] This means that every time we apply the Weird technique we have around a one in 10 chance that we'll actually be dreaming.

Look closely and check the facts

No reality check technique works 100 per cent of the time, and not every dream is full of obvious dream signs, so what can you do if your hand doesn't change but you're still sure you're dreaming? How can you spot a dream sign if the dreamscape is seemingly devoid of them? Well, you can bring out your notepad, scrunch up one eye and say, 'And one more thing...'

Think back, if you can, to the 70s TV homicide detective named Lieutenant Columbo. This guy didn't have flashy forensics, he just possessed a sharp mind that took in every detail of the environment while checking the facts and looking closely. That's just how we need to be if we want to solve the mystery of the lucid dream.

Five steps to becoming Columbo

The Columbo Method is fundamentally based on looking closely. Here's how to do it:

1. If you think you might be dreaming, scan the area for clues and touch things. The dream state looks amazingly realistic, but if you look closely enough you'll often be able to see inconsistencies and realize that you're dreaming.

2. Be mindful and ask yourself, *How did I get here? Where was I before? What's the last thing I can remember?*

3. To really empower the Columbo method, practise it in the daytime, too. As you go through your daily life, or perhaps for a designated 10 minutes a day, look very closely at things, explore the texture of your surroundings and search for evidence of dreamlike phenomena.

4. When practising the daytime Columbo method, every time your investigation leads to a new discovery (*I expected the bark on this tree to feel different*) and you think, *That's weird,* be sure to do a reality check. Soon you'll end up doing this in your dreams too.

5. We dream as we live so by bringing mindful awareness into everyday life we will become more mindfully aware in our dreams too.

Tips from the pros: Becoming a detective of life, with Daniel Love

Stay lucid

The primary mystery we're attempting to solve is the question, 'Am I dreaming?', but this is an ongoing adventure with many other avenues to explore. We must attempt to stay lucid in every area of our life – both waking and dreaming – if we are truly to solve the mystery.

Use your tools

As any detective will tell you, to get to the truth of a matter you'll need to employ certain mental tools. Educate yourself in the skills of awareness, critical thinking, logic, deduction, mindfulness and data gathering, as these should all become part of your detective's toolkit. As with muscles, the more you exercise these skills, the stronger they will become.

Question everything

While it's often easier to accept things at face value, remember this is exactly the kind of lazy thinking that leads to non-lucid dreams. So question what you're told, question your own assumptions, question the facts, question everything.

Increase your knowledge

Get into the habit of looking for answers and searching for facts. Treat life like a classroom, full of new things to learn. Be prepared to discover new ways of thinking and occasionally to throw out old ideas. As a side effect, you'll also become a far more interesting person.

Search for clues

As a detective of life, you'll need a keen eye and a thirst for evidence, as you'll never be quite sure where the trail of clues will eventually lead. Becoming aware that you're dreaming is only the tip of the iceberg and, if you choose, it may be the start of an adventure that can open your mind to the kaleidoscopic wonder of the universe.

Daniel Love is the author of *Are You Dreaming?* Visit www.exploringluciddreams.com for more information about his work.

CHARLIE'S TOOLBOX CHECKLIST ✍

- ❖ If you're in a dream and you know that you're dreaming that's great, but if you need an extra indicator to let yourself know that you're *definitely* dreaming (before you go and fly off that cliff!) then do a reality check in the dream.

- ❖ Do reality checks while you're awake too (10 a day or more if you can), whenever you see something weird or dreamlike.

- ❖ Be like Columbo and look closely at life. You've got about 100 years max to do your thing so don't waste it by experiencing the world in tunnel vision! Broaden your awareness and see just how dreamy 'real life' actually is. By doing this soon you'll notice how dreamy your dream life is too.

- ❖ Don't forget to keep up the dream diary and the dream-sign spotting!

Part II

GOING
DEEPER

'Trust in dreams, for in them is
the hidden gate to eternity.'
KHALIL GIBRAN

Chapter 4
Archetypes, nightmares and the shadow

While observing his clients, the great Swiss psychiatrist Carl Jung noticed that although they would often dream about their daily lives, the content of their dreams and fantasies was not just limited to their everyday experiences. He saw that they'd often enter into a realm of ancient symbolism, about which they'd had no conscious pre-acquired knowledge.

Their dreams and fantasies often contained mythological themes that existed in cultures they'd never visited and in times before the birth of any of their relatives. This observation led Jung to formulate his concept of 'archetypes' and the collective unconscious, two of his major contributions to psychology.

Archetypes and the collective unconscious

Jung saw that certain dream content was transpersonal, sourced not from our own *personal unconscious* but from what he termed the *collective unconscious*: a vast storehouse of ancient human experience containing themes and images found cross-culturally throughout history. The collective unconscious has been described as 'an attic of ancient volumes of cherished memories from the history of all humankind',[1] which is part of us all.

Jung called the themes that emerged from the timeless realms of the collective unconscious 'archetypes'. Archetypes are symbolic representations of universally existing aspects of the unconscious mind. They are what 'make up the contents of the collective unconscious and have a powerful effect on the individual,' because their function is as a form of communication from the unconscious to the conscious mind.[2]

Theoretically, there's an infinite number of archetypes, but there are some that show up in people's dreams so often that they've become mainstays of Jungian psychology. Each archetype is 'more of a theme than a specifically determined thing',[3] but there are certain themes that seem to appear in every mind, in every part of the world.

Some of the most frequently encountered archetypes are the wise man (representing guidance, knowledge, wisdom), the mother (nurturing, comforting, feminine), the Self or higher self[4] (inner unification) and the shadow (unacceptable psychological content).[5] Jung believed that archetypes 'transcend the personal psychology of the dreamer'[6] and point to something much bigger, and more universal. He said that 'whenever a phenomenon is found to be characteristic of all human communities, it's an expression of an archetype of the collective unconscious.'[7]

Strange but true

Carl Jung didn't just change the world of psychology, he also had a huge but often overlooked influence on language. Commonly used terms such as introvert and extrovert, complex, and archetype are words and concepts that Jung himself either invented or popularized. He even gave a name to the times when our external environment resonates with our psychological process to such a degree that it results in a meaningful coincidence – he called this synchronicity.

Meeting the shadow

One of the unique aspects of lucid dreaming is that in a lucid dream we can actually meet and interact with our internal archetypes, which will often appear in personified form. This means that we can encounter these powerful representations of our own psychology in a very real way, make friends with them and step into the powerful energy that they contain. This is one of the most amazing potentials of lucid dreaming.

We can, of course, connect with these inner archetypes in the waking state too - through visualizations, active imagination and hypnosis, for example - but however deeply we go into these practices, there will very rarely be a personified manifestation of the archetype standing in front of us, ready to converse. In a lucid dream, though, there may well be, because once lucid you can actually *meet* your inner child, have a conversation with your wise man, and even encounter the energy of your higher self, 'the archetype of archetypes'.

Jung believed that meeting your higher self would allow you to 'communicate directly with the ageless, cellular wisdom held within the hidden dimensions of your mind',[8] but my favourite archetype to work with in the lucid dream state is the shadow.

The shadow is a Jungian concept used to describe the parts of the unconscious mind made up of all the undesirable aspects of our psyche that we've rejected, disowned, repressed or denied. It's what the poet Robert Bly called 'the bag that we drag behind us', and it's comprised of everything within us that we don't want to face: our traumas, our fears, taboos, perversions and much more.

It has been said that the shadow is the only archetype we're not born with. We create our shadow, every time we repress or deny an unacceptable part of ourselves. This begins in childhood, often with the shaming of our own nakedness as we realize that being naked is frowned upon. Many of us received the message 'my naked body is bad' and so we disown our nakedness and force it into the shadowy 'cellar of the unacceptable' where it's soon joined by other objectionable qualities such as anger and greed, both of which we're taught are unbefitting for 'good' little boys and girls to display.

Your shadow is most obviously revealed in your dreams and nightmares, and one way you can integrate its content is by becoming lucid and literally embracing it. Embracing your shadow once lucid will allow you to integrate your 'dark side', transmute its energy and move through your limitations into a space of deep psychological balance.

Strange but true

Although the shadow is often thought of in negative terms, we also have a positive shadow: positive traits within us that we're unwilling to accept as being part of us. For example, being a great dancer or having lots of charisma may have been seen as unacceptable to us when we were children, so we pushed them into the shadows. As adults we might find that these positive expressions of shadow content reveal themselves as we start psychological work.

Those of you who've seen my TED talk will know that I love working with the shadow. It's often misinterpreted as some sort of evil or demonic presence that's both separate from us and harmful, leading us to waste the valuable learning process it offers by investing our energy in ways to defeat it. But the truth is that the shadow is neither external nor harmful. It's simply our *dark side* – a 'reservoir for human darkness' – but an aspect of our selves which, as Jung commented, forms 'the seat of all creativity'.[9]

The shadow is part of us and until we accept that its darkness doesn't come from an external 'evil' but from a wellspring of internal creative energy, we'll never become fully integrated human beings. As my teacher Rob Nairn once told me: 'The shadow is such good news!'

This process of engaging shadow aspects with the aim of integrating and assimilating them into the self is part of what Jung called 'individuation' – the move towards psychological wholeness. This is one of the highest aims of psychological work, so we can see how lucid dreaming offers us an arena in which to connect with such deep levels of our psyche that when we wake in the morning, we may feel very different from the day before. Through shadow integration we transform what we thought was a demon into what it was all along – our divine spirit, or what used to be known as our daemon.

A psychotherapist friend of mine heard me talk about this recently and was shocked by this potential. He told me, 'It can take months of therapy to get to the stage where a client even acknowledges internal archetypes like the shadow and the inner child, let alone actually meet personifications of them in a lucid dream! This stuff could change everything.'

Wanna go deeper?

To explore your personal shadow, take a moment to think about the parts of yourself that you find unacceptable to show to others. Aspects of your sexuality that you fear may be frowned upon, perhaps. Or your anger, or your past traumas. Or maybe it's your great singing voice, or your innate intelligence, which you dare not show for fear of seeming 'too clever'? If there is a part of you that you don't want to accept or show to others then you can be sure that it makes up an aspect of your shadow.

For more information on the shadow and how to work directly with it through dreams, see *Dreams of Awakening*.

Let's learn how to meet that particularly misunderstood archetype now, shall we? But before we do we need to learn about its home turf: nightmares.

Lucid nightmares

Have you ever had a nightmare in which you've thought, *Wake up! I want to wake up!*? If so, that nightmare was a lucid dream, because by wanting to wake yourself up you indirectly acknowledged that there was a place to wake up to. Nightmares are great for lucid dreaming, and for many people (more than a third of those surveyed) their first taste of lucid dreaming came about through nightmares or anxiety dreams.

But why should nightmares so often lead to lucidity? Imagine this: if I somehow managed to travel through the pages of this book and jump out into your lap you'd probably be so frightened that your eyes would widen, your mind would become sharpened and you'd definitely become more alert, right? (I hope you'd then start looking at your hands and ask, 'Am I dreaming?' too.)

Research has shown that the boost of awareness that fear brings is an evolutionary trait that helps us deal with a potential threat, so when we feel scared or threatened in our dreams our awareness is similarly boosted, which can often lead to the fully conscious awareness of lucidity.

For some people, chronic nightmares are a serious complaint that not only affects the quality of their sleep, but also the quality of their lives. The good news, though, is that if you can experience a nightmare with full lucidity, you have a powerful opportunity for trauma resolution and shadow integration.

I've taught lucid dreaming to numerous people suffering from post-traumatic stress disorder – including ex-soldiers, victims of terrorist attacks and those who experienced abuse during childhood – and I've seen first-hand just how powerful lucid dream training can be, not only in curing nightmares but more importantly in opening people up to a new perspective of sleep and dreams in which they see their nightmares as a call for help rather than an attack from the unconscious.

The science bit

There's hard science to back up all this stuff too. A 1997 study, which took five people suffering from chronic nightmares and taught them to lucid dream, concluded that 'the alleviation of recurrent nightmares was effective in all five cases' and that 'treatments based on lucid dream induction can be of therapeutic value'.[10] A follow-up study one year later showed that 'four of the five subjects no longer had nightmares and that the other experienced a decrease in the intensity and frequency of her nightmares.'[11]

A 2006 study entitled 'Lucid dreaming for treatment of nightmares' concluded that 'lucid dream training seems effective in reducing nightmare frequency',[12] and at the 2009 European Science Foundation meeting it was stated that lucid dreaming is such an effective remedy for nightmares that people have the potential to be 'treated by training to dream lucidly'.[13]

And finally a 2013 neurobiological study from Brazil concluded that lucid dreaming could be used 'as a therapy for post-traumatic stress disorder.'[14]

Sadly, there's been no follow-up on this treatment option for recurrent nightmares. So if we have all this research indicating that lucid dreaming can cure nightmares, why isn't it being offered by mainstream medicine? Maybe it's because the training needed to teach people to have lucid dreams is beyond the remit of current health-care providers, or perhaps it's because the use of a freely available method like lucid dreaming isn't attractive to the big companies who profit from medicating the thousands of chronic nightmares suffers.

I'm lucid in my nightmare, what now?

The first thing most people do when they become lucid in a nightmare is try to wake themselves up. This seems logical, but it's actually missing a valuable opportunity, because when you do that, the mental trauma or anxiety that's causing the nightmare, and the shadow content, remains unintegrated and so the nightmare may well recur.

My advice is this: if you're lucky enough to become lucidly aware within a nightmare, try to *stay in the nightmare* for as long as you can, reminding yourself that it's all just a projection of your own mind and that nothing in the nightmare can do you harm. Many people find that by shifting their perspective like this they can actually create a total transformation of attitude that tells the nightmare: 'I see you, and I understand that you're an expression of my own mind that just wants to be seen.'

The paradox is that by looking directly at the nightmare it doesn't grow under your gaze, it actually diminishes. By shining light into the darkness and revealing the source of a shadow, we see that the source is often much smaller than the shadow it casts.

The nightmare doesn't mean to hurt us – it means to grab our attention and show us which aspects of our mind need healing. In many cases a nightmare is just a dream that's shouting, 'Hey, look at this! Deal with this! This needs attention!' and it will shout louder and louder, over and over until you turn to face it, listen to it and bear witness to its display, with compassionate acceptance.

Once the nightmare has received this message of acceptance it'll often dissolve spontaneously and never return. Why? Because as we learned earlier 'the seeing is the doing' and so by simply bearing witness to the nightmare, without judgement and knowing that it's an unintegrated expression of our own shadow (rather than some externalized demon), its energy will be accepted and integrated.

There's another option too: once lucid, rather than just acknowledging the nightmare we can proactively embrace it. For example, if the source of our nightmare was a man in a black hood chasing us, we could actually move towards him and hug him within the dream – a hug being the ultimate symbolic expression of full acceptance. (If the source of the nightmare was a feeling rather than a thing then our acceptance and embrace would simply be engaged through our intent).

And then there's the third option – to call forth your shadow aspects intentionally. How? By using a non-nightmarish lucid dream as a place to actually invoke your shadow in order to bear witness to it, have a dialogue with it, and of course, give it a hug.

Strange but true

The ancient Mesopotamians had a very down-to-earth way of dealing with nightmares. They would tell their frightening dreams to a lump of clay that had been rubbed over their body. The clay would then be thrown into water, where it would dissolve, along with the energetic residue of the nightmare.[15]

Isn't all this shadow-hugging stuff a bit dangerous? No, in fact it's far more dangerous *not* to move towards acceptance of the shadow, because by allowing it to fester in our denial it will grow and become more powerfully removed from the rest of the psyche. The longer things stay in the shadows the darker and denser they become, and yet, once we're ready to shine light into the places that scare us, we can unravel decades of darkness in one lucid dream.

This was something that the subject of our next case study discovered when she finally decided to hug the source of her nightmares.

Case study: Hugging the shadow

Dreamer: *Kerri, South Africa*

Age: *34*

The lowdown from Kerri: *'I was playing a game of avoidance with myself. I was feeling sterile and hard. I was in complete denial about the crippled little girl within me who was so desperate for love, and wanted to feel safe. I would put myself in painful, humiliating and unsafe situations to try to prove that I was strong so I wouldn't have to look at the small child inside, crying to be seen. I did everything to avoid the truth about myself.'*

Kerri's dream report: *'In the dream I was standing in my lounge when I noticed a frightening-looking figure, dressed in black, creeping along the window. He was trying to break in. He began violently smashing against the window. I recoiled against the wall, terrified, as I watched the intruder gain entry. He ran towards me; I believed he wanted to attack, harm and kill me. He was the sum total of my worst fears. The terror of this nightmare charged me into lucidity.*

'Once lucid I was able to recognize that this man was an aspect of my shadow. I knew that I had to go and hug him. As I held him I felt repulsion and terror; he felt oily and disgusting. It felt so wrong to be hugging a person like this but I kept hugging him and saying the Tibetan compassion mantra Om mani peme hung *like a plea.*

'Suddenly he began to shrink in my arms, growing smaller and smaller until he slipped out of them. When I finally plucked up the courage to look down, I saw that he'd transformed into a small child, just a baby. He was lying in the foetal position at my feet and was sobbing. I suddenly felt such compassion for him and I bent down towards his little body and started to chant Om mani peme hung *to him again. The dream dissolved and I felt a strong wind move through me, which felt like pure joy. I woke up crying with bliss.'*

Life since the dream: *'This dream helped me to see that what I cannot accept in myself gets left to mutate and grow to such an extent that it eventually becomes the most frightening and threatening "external" thing, but actually it was only ever my unresolved stuff. The* *attacking monster was actually the crippled little girl in me that I could never accept. The dream showed me how orphans of our consciousness – in my case the neglected child who never felt loved – could become powerful monsters over time.*

'*After this dream I just felt different. I tried to begin to live more lucidly, especially in areas of conflict and fear. I began facing my difficulties instead of running away. I decided to heal estrangements in my life, to move towards them and embrace them, just as I'd done in the dream. The most significant of these estrangements that I healed concerned my father, whom I hadn't spoken to for a few years. Today our relationship is healed and sometimes we even chant* Om mani peme hung *together.*'

Kerri's dream is a wonderful example of how to embrace the shadow. It shows how even the parts of ourselves that seem terrifying are often simply unintegrated aspects that are shouting to be heard. Once they're given the attention they need, and we can bear witness to their energy with acceptance, they'll usually reveal themselves to us fully and completely, as they've been waiting to do all along.

Lucid dream shadow integration is a deeply healing psycho-spiritual practice that you can do in your sleep. It sounds almost too good to be true, right? But it *is* true and it *is* doable – by each and every one of us, if we only take the time to learn how. So let's carry on learning how with our next toolbox, which contains some of my all-time favourite techniques.

🧰 TOOLBOX 4: MOVING INTO LUCIDITY

Now that you've begun to look closely at your dreams, and (hopefully) started to apply methods such as reality checks and the Weird technique, you might find that you're starting to get some flashes of lucidity in the formerly unlit space of your dreamtime. So before we go any further let's explore just what this might look like.

The lucidity spectrum

The dawning of lucidity is not always a light-bulb moment; in fact it's often more of a dimmer switch that slowly fades up, gradually illuminating our minds to the possibility that we're dreaming. There's a whole spectrum of lucidity based on varying degrees of conscious awareness within the dream, ranging from a suspicion that we might be dreaming to absolute knowledge that everything we're experiencing is mind.

I tend to work with four main levels of lucidity, although this is a very basic system of categorization and it's not necessary to stick to it rigidly. Our transition through the lucidity spectrum is not always a linear one either, and although level 1 may often lead to level 2, and so on, it's also common to find ourselves at level 3 or 4 straight away, thanks to a sudden light-bulb moment of awareness.

The four levels of lucidity

Level 1: Pre-lucid

This is the state of mind in which we begin critically questioning the reality of the dream. In the pre-lucid state, suspicions arise that we might be dreaming, usually after we've become aware of some bizarre dream anomaly.

Level 2: Semi-lucid

On this level we experience the 'Aha!' moment of lucid awareness, but then slip back and forth between lucidity and non-lucidity. We may be lucid one moment, and then become distracted by the dream and slip back into non-lucidity. We can also use this term to describe a low level of lucid awareness.

Level 3: Fully lucid

This is the state of fully conscious reflective awareness within the dream, coupled with volitional interaction with the dreamscape and dream characters. Essentially, this means that we're fully aware that we're dreaming and can begin to direct the dream at will: we can choose to fly, we can choose to meet our shadow and so on. Many people believe that this is the highest level of lucidity, but there's one more to go.

Level 4: Super-lucid

This is a term borrowed from lucid dream explorers Robert Waggoner and Ed Kellogg to describe the state in which we have a level of awareness that surpasses full lucidity, due to an experience of partial non-dual awareness.

What does this mean? Well, the fundamental difference between 'fully lucid' and 'super-lucid' rests on a subtle but profound shift of perception. Most of us experiencing a fully lucid dream will interact with the dream as if it's waking reality, using doors to leave rooms and flying though the sky to get somewhere.

While super-lucid, however, we base all our actions on the realization that everything in the dream is a creation of mind. We realize that we don't need to fly anywhere, we can just arrive there instantly, and that walls are just as easy to walk through as doors.

Witnessing dream

This type of dream falls within the lucidity spectrum but it doesn't quite fit into any of the four levels described above. We experience a witnessing dream from a gentle, non-preferential perspective, fully aware that we're dreaming but without any desire to influence or interact with the dream. Instead we allow it to unfold on its own, often as though we're watching it on a movie screen.

Don't worry too much about the different levels of lucidity. I've included the lucidity spectrum here more as a way to explore the dynamics and nature of lucidity, rather than make it a cornerstone of the practice.

Now that we know just how lucid we can become, let's learn some powerful methods for inducing it!

Hypnagogic affirmation

Now that you know what the hypnagogic state is, I'm pretty sure you can imagine how this technique works. As you fall asleep through the hypnagogic state, mentally recite a positive affirmation of your intent to gain lucidity. As we've learned, the hypnagogic state is very similar to the hypnotic state, so if we apply a suggestion or affirmation within it, we may find that it has the potential to work with hypnotic effect.

Five steps to hypnagogic affirmation

You can do this technique as you first fall asleep at night, but for best results practise it after an early-hours wake-up about 5 or 6 hours after you went to bed. At this time the hypnagogic will lead directly into the dream state. Whenever you practise it though, the important thing is to saturate your sleepy consciousness with the strong aspiration to have a lucid dream. Here's how:

1. Take some time to create an affirmation of your intent to have a lucid dream such as, 'I recognize my dreams with full lucidity' or 'Next time I dream, I know that I'm dreaming', or whatever phrase you feel best encapsulates your intention to get lucid.

2. As you enter the hypnagogic state, continuously recite this affirmation in your mind.

3. Try to recite your affirmation with real feeling and gusto – this is vital, because without determination, this technique simply won't work.

4. The important thing is not so much that you're repeating the affirmation right up to the point at which you enter the dream (although that would be great), but more that you saturate your last few minutes of conscious awareness with the strong intention to gain lucidity.

5. Aim for your affirmation to be the last thing to pass through your mind before you black out.

LaBerge's Mnemonic Induction of Lucid Dreams

For an upgrade of the hypnagogic affirmation technique, check out MILD (mnemonic induction of lucid dreams), which is one of the most well-known lucidity techniques out there. The guy who formulated it, Stephen LaBerge, is an American scientist who was one of the pioneers of lucid dreaming back in the early 80s. LaBerge used this technique to give himself lucid dreams at will, almost every single night.

Mnemonic means 'pertaining to memory' and a mnemonic-induced lucid dream is one that works by using the function of memory. MILD is based upon three core principles:

❖ Visualization

❖ Autosuggestion (self-hypnosis)

❖ Prospective memory

Although visualization and autosuggestion provide the foundational power of this technique, it's prospective memory that provides the real crux. We use prospective memory all the time in our daily life – when we say things like, 'Next time I see a bank I'll remember to get out some cash,' and it's actually a very reliable aspect of memory.

If we set a prospective memory command as we fall asleep – 'Next time I'm dreaming I'll remember to recognize that I'm dreaming' – it'll stay neurologically engaged until we 'see the bank' as it were and find ourselves dreaming.

The MILD technique

This is a technique that requires us to visualize ourselves back in the dream that we were just having and so it's best practised after waking from a vividly recalled dream. This can be done naturally, perhaps when you've woken up in the early hours, or intentionally, by setting an alarm to wake yourself up during a REM period some time in the last few hours of your sleep cycle.

Step 1: Recalling the dream

After awakening from a period of dreaming, wake up fully and recall the dream that you were just having. Learn the basic plot and scenario off by heart. You'll find out why in step 3.

Step 2: Setting the intent

Now get ready to go back to sleep. As you begin to fall asleep and enter the hypnagogic state, mentally recite over and over again, with determination and enthusiasm: *The next time I'm dreaming, I remember to recognize that I'm dreaming.* Focus on this command and if you feel your mind start to wander, or realize that it's wandered already, just bring yourself back to the recitation.

Step 3: Visualizing lucidity

Once you've created and stabilized the strong motivation to *remember to recognize that you're dreaming*, the next step is to visualize yourself back in the dream that you recalled earlier. Really try to relive it in as much detail as you can, envisaging yourself back in it and experiencing it with all your senses as you drift off to sleep.

However, this time, imagine that you recognize that you're dreaming and become fully lucid. How? By imagining yourself spotting a dream sign or doing a reality check and then having the realization, *Aha! I'm dreaming!*

Then imagine acting out what you might like to do once you're lucid.

Step 4: Drop off to sleep or Do it again

Now you can either just fall asleep or repeat steps 2 and 3 again until you feel sure that you've fully engaged the technique, at which point you can drop the technique and allow yourself to fall asleep.

Here's an easy way to remember the order of the MILD technique:

M: Memorize the dream you were just having
I: set the **I**ntent
L: visualize **L**ucidity
D: Drop off to sleep or **D**o it again.

For a full explanation of this technique, see *Exploring the World of Lucid Dreaming* by Dr Stephen LaBerge.

Strange but true

It appears that the MILD technique, along with many other Western lucid dream methods, was not invented in the twentieth century, but rather in medieval Tibet. An almost identical technique to MILD can be found in a sixteenth-century dream yoga text by a Tibetan Lama named Lochen Dharma Shri.[16]

Wake, back to bed technique

This technique can boost your chances of having a lucid dream by a whopping 2,000 per cent'[17], and more than two-thirds of research participants recorded lucid dreams when engaging in this practice.[18] So how do we practise this supercharged technique? It's simple. Wake up at least two hours earlier than normal, stay awake for about an hour and then go back to sleep for another hour or two. Here's how:

Five steps to wake, back to bed

1. Set your alarm for at least two hours earlier than your usual wake-up time.

2. When the alarm sounds, wake up and get out of bed.

3. Stay awake for about an hour, engaging in any fully wakeful activity. Meditating or reading about lucid dreaming is ideal, but I've found that just about any mindful activity works well.

4. You want to be awake but not wired, so don't overstimulate yourself or you might find step five a bit tricky. Try to keep sleep at arm's reach.

5. After about an hour, reset your alarm for an hour or two later, return to bed and fall asleep again with the strong intention to gain lucidity. You can mentally recite a lucidity affirmation too, if you like.

How does wake, back to bed work?

As we've learned, the last two hours of our sleep cycle are when we do most of our dreaming, so if we starve ourselves of this dream time, when we go back to sleep we eventually course smoothly and deeply into vivid dreaming. As dreaming sleep is the playing field for lucidity, we can see how this technique puts us well on the winning side.

Simply wake up a couple of hours earlier than usual, stay awake for an hour and then go back to sleep with a strong intent to become lucid.

Now that we're really getting stuck into the techniques let's have some more general tips on getting lucid from Luigi Sciambarella, representing the UK branch of the Monroe Institute.

Tips from the pros: Getting lucid, with Luigi Sciambarella

Be well rested and physically relaxed
If you're sleep deprived, the first thing your brain/body will focus on is clawing back sleep debt. You'll plunge into sleep too quickly to control your awareness and you're unlikely to remember many dreams. Ideally, you should be getting at least 7½ hours of sleep per night. It's often useful to go to bed a little earlier than normal in order to have time to set the intention to have a lucid dream.

Improve your dream recall
Lucid dreams are remarkable and often life-changing experiences, but without conscious effort to remember the content, you might forget significant parts of the experience. You can start by keeping a dream diary next to your bed at night and setting the intention to write your dreams down in the morning when you wake up.

Be more present in the daytime and think ahead
Meditation practices, such as breath awareness, can help to keep you in the present during the day. This will start to carry through into your dreaming. For lucid dreaming, it's very important to develop your prospective memory so set yourself memory challenges throughout the day.

Set a strong intention
Apathy is lucid dreaming's biggest killer so it's important to keep an eye on your motivation levels. Think about why you want to lucid dream, and what you're going to accomplish on your next

exploration. The more you think about having a lucid dream, the more likely it is to occur so take time to read about and reflect upon the benefits of lucid dreaming as you go about your day.

Have fun!

This is your playground: a fertile soil where you can grow new patterns and weed out those that no longer serve you. It's most productive to approach the task of self-exploration in an open, light-hearted manner. Too much intense effort is often counterproductive, and being too critical of yourself over unsuccessful attempts can quickly lead to anger, frustration and apathy, so remember to keep a sense of humour about it all.

Visit www.monroeinstituteuk.org for more info on Luigi's lucid dream and Out of Body Exploration courses.

CHARLIE'S TOOLBOX CHECKLIST ✍

❖ Get to know the lucidity spectrum experientially. Intentionally explore the pre-lucid, semi-lucid, fully lucid, super-lucid and witnessing states.

❖ Once a week, be sure to schedule a morning to practise the wake back to bed technique, perhaps on a weekend or a day when you don't have to be at work the next day.

❖ Have a go at writing your own hypnagogic affirmations and experiment with what works best for you. This is one of my personal favourites: 'I love lucid dreaming. Lucid dreaming's lots of fun.' It's so confident yet playful that even the most hardened unconscious will take note.

❖ Decide which technique to do *before* you go to bed, rather than trying to pick one when you're half asleep. Maybe spend a few nights getting to know the MILD technique and then schedule in a wake, back to bed session at the weekend. Be creative but disciplined!

❖ Don't forget to keep up the reality checks and Columbo mindset in the daytime, as well as practising these new toolbox techniques at night.

Chapter 5

Lucid dreaming around the world – Greeks, geeks and the Columbus of Hull

Let's take a look now at some of the various lucid dreaming traditions around the world – both historical and present-day – which take us from semi-mythical experience to scientifically verified fact. The world's a big place and this is a small book, so I won't attempt a chronological study of them all, but I'll try to give you a flavour of a few key ones, starting with those found in the West.

The ancient Greeks

The first substantial venture into dream work in Europe came, unsurprisingly, from the ancient Greeks. Aristotle famously wrote about lucid dreaming in his treatise *On Dreams*, saying: 'when one is asleep, there's something in consciousness which tells us that what presents itself is but a dream.'[1]

The ancient Greeks even had purpose-built temples in which people would spend the night engaging in specific dream incubation techniques, hoping for a dream of healing. In the fifth century BCE, Greece had at least 350 temples dedicated to healing and most of these had specific areas dedicated to healing dream work.[2]

The dreamers would fall asleep on stone beds while incense burners diffused the smoke of what may have been psychoactive herbs to aid dreaming. Thanks to the dozens of positive testimonials inscribed onto the temples' walls[3] we can assume that the dream-work techniques being practised were overwhelmingly effective.

When the Romans arrived in Britain in AD43, they brought with them many of the dream traditions they'd absorbed from the Greeks. Consequently there was even a dream temple built in what is now Gloucestershire in the southwest of England. The ruins of this temple are still visible today and they've been studied extensively by contemporary British dream researchers Paul and Charla Devereux, who have even run guided tours around them.

Strange but true

One of the weirdest aspects of the Greek dream temples was the use of non-venomous snakes to lick the eyelids of those hoping for a dream of healing. The priests in Britain's dream temples had to adapt to local conditions, though – they used dogs to lick the patients' eyelids instead![4]

Early and Medieval Christians

The original Christians were quite open to dream work (it was, after all, a series of dreams that heralded Jesus's birth). The early gnostic Christians even used the metaphor of the lucid dream as one of their central images for unity with God, and in the fifth century Greek bishops would tell people that while they dream, 'the soul is taken to a superior region where it can come in contact with true things'.[5] After the fifth century however, things start to go downhill fast for Christian dreamers.

One of the most ardent of these downhill enthusiasts was the man who became St Jerome – a Latin Christian priest who had a dream that had far-reaching consequences. In it he was given a message to stop studying the pagan literature that so fascinated him. Many of these texts were about dream work and so he interpreted this message to mean that he should turn his back on dream work as a whole.

It just so happens that St Jerome was also one of the first translators of the Bible into Latin. His prejudice against dream work was reflected in his fifth-century translation, as he selectively mistranslated many passages mentioning witchcraft as also mentioning dream work. Suddenly the Bible was full of passages saying that working with dreams is wrong,[6] and with that, the history of dreaming within Christian culture changed forever.

Then in the thirteenth century the influential Christian philosopher Thomas Aquinas suggested that 'some dreams come from demons'[7] and in the 1500s Jesuit priests even said that 'the devil is most always implicated in dreams'.[8]

Due to these opinions, and those of many more influential Christians, by the end of the medieval era dream work within Christianity was lost for good. However, its revival is well underway with thousands of Christians around the world today using lucid dreaming to further their relationship to God. Amen to that.

The nineteenth and twentieth centuries

The traditions we've explored so far were engaging dream practices, but they weren't primarily *lucid* dream practices. It's not until the nineteenth and twentieth centuries that we get the first major outings into Western public consciousness of the concept of lucid dreaming.

It was a Frenchman, the Marquis d'Hervey de Saint Denys, who, with the publication of his 1867 book *Dreams and How to Guide them*, offered the first publicly available book on the subject of lucid dreaming. The work contained chapters on increasing dream recall, being aware of dreaming, awakening at will and conscious interaction with the dream narrative: a pretty comprehensive lucid dreaming guide which is still relevant today. The marquis' dream record covered 1,946 nights of practice and was a thorough exploration of the potentials of lucidity.

Then, in the early 1900s, the term 'lucid dream' was popularized by the Dutch psychiatrist Frederik Willems van Eden, in part due to his 1913 presentation to the Society for Psychical Research in which he reported 352 documented 'lucid dreams'. Up until that point a variety of other descriptions, such as 'half dreams' or 'guided dreams', were used to describe the phenomenon of conscious awareness within the dream state, a phenomenon which wasn't to be verified by Western science until the mid-1970s.

Freud and Jung

In 1900 came Sigmund Freud's seminal work, *The Interpretation of Dreams*. Although it contained only a few passing references to lucid dreaming (and even those are only in later editions) it made an indelible impression in both public and scientific circles of the importance of dream work. The book opened up the possibility that dreams were beneficial, and that to understand them and be aware of them was something to be recommended.

Freud was so interested in the phenomenon of lucid dreaming that he reportedly tried to get hold of a copy of the Marquis d'Hervey de Saint Denys' *Dreams and How to Guide them*, but was unable to do so.[9] Imagine how different the path of lucid dreaming might have been had he managed to obtain the book, and perhaps even trained himself to lucid dream? With so much of Freud's work being based on personal experience we can postulate that if he'd practised lucid dreaming the general public would have become aware of the phenomenon more than 60 years sooner, and would have perhaps even been encouraged to practise it.

Then came Carl Jung, the one-time student of Freud, whose work we looked at in Chapter 4. Jung felt that Freud had merely scratched the surface of the dream world: he came to believe that the sexual symbolism in dreams – on which Freud placed such emphasis – was often obscuring deeper, non-sexual, spiritual meanings and psychic functions. As we learned earlier Jung introduced the ideas of archetypes and the collective unconscious, which would lay the foundation for an entire movement of transpersonal dream work in which lucid dreaming would find a home.

Throughout the early twentieth century a growing wave of curiosity, fuelled by Western interest in dreams, orientalism and esoteric thought, led to the publication of an array of studies and personal accounts of lucid dreaming by occultist and esoteric writers. Many of these publications are being revisited and republished today and I encourage you to seek them out if you can.

Scientific trailblazers

The first major scientific advancement in the study of dreaming came in 1924, with the invention of a skull cap that could record electrical activity in the human brain through electrode sensors placed in contact with the subject's scalp. This device would gather a record of brain-wave activity that became known as electroencephalography, or EEG. It was these EEG recordings of the brain in sleep that would provide the bedrock for all subsequent research into sleep, and even the final evidence that lucid dreaming was science fact, not fiction.

Then, in 1953, just as the structure of DNA was being unravelled, the structure of sleep and dreaming was being unravelled too, as a graduate student at the University of Chicago named Eugene Aserinsky discovered and verified the existence of REM sleep.

For the preceding couple of years Aserinsky had been struggling financially, in both his personal and academic life. Sleep science was viewed with indifference by most of the scientific community and so he'd been unable to attract funding for his research project. Without funding the indomitable sleep geek ended up finding and fixing an abandoned EEG machine and began conducting studies on his eight-year-old son[10] (the only volunteer he could find who would accept sweets as payment).

Young Armand Aserinsky was hooked up to the EEG machine and eventually fell asleep while his father watched his brain activity from an adjacent room. For the first 70 minutes or so Armand's brain wasn't doing much, but soon it began to display activation similar to that of a waking brain. As his brain became active the boy's eyes began to twitch under their lids, a phenomenon which soon became known as rapid eye movement. Aserinsky had just discovered REM dreaming sleep.

REM sleep is the phase of sleep in which the brain is actively engaged in creating our dreams, while the body is put into a state of muscle paralysis to stop us acting them out. During REM sleep the body is switched off while the brain is switched on, and its core principle is its direct correlation to the experience of dreaming.

The reason why the discovery of REM sleep was so instrumental in the scientific exploration and validation of dreams is that it provided the first substantiated connection between the objective measurements of neurological and optical activity with the subjective reports of those experiencing dreaming sleep. Finally, it was proven that dreams could be objectively measured, as well as subjectively described – criteria that would then be applied to the task of proving lucid dreaming some 20 years later.

And what of Eugene Aserinsky? Strangely, rather than continue to move down the trail that he'd so far blazed, he chose to leave the University of Chicago to study the effects of electrical currents on salmon.[11] Weird, eh? (I hope you're doing a reality check.)

A few years later, in 1959, the first scientific studies into lucid dreaming began. A favourable 1940s report by the US psychiatrist Nathan Rapport inspired researchers at Goethe University in Germany to conduct a study in which they taught people how to lucid dream and then observed them as they were dreaming and became lucid.[12]

This study was pretty much ignored by the scientific establishment and, up until the mid-1970s, lucid dreaming was still scoffed at by most scientists. They believed it was a 'paradoxical impossibility' that had no credible data to support its validity. However, following the 1968 publication of Celia Green's *Lucid Dreams* (one of the first scholarly studies of the practice) and then Patricia Garfield's popular *Creative Dreaming* in 1974, the foundation stones were starting to be laid for that special day in 1975 when something amazing happened: lucid dreaming was scientifically verified.

The Columbus of Hull University

In some scientific circles, there's an almost religious belief that until science *proves* the existence of something, it simply *doesn't* exist. This was presumably the same attitude that some people had towards the Americas before Columbus 'discovered' them and made a continent with millennia of rich history suddenly 'exist'.

So too it was with lucid dreaming. Thousands of years of documented experience, and a whole faculty of Tibetan Buddhism dedicated to its research, were dismissed as 'non-existent' until science could prove lucid dreaming on its own terms. Up until the mid-1970s, many had tried but none had managed to convince the scientific establishment that being conscious within a dream was for real. That was until one man at Hull University in the UK set out to prove empirically what he already knew to be true.

The man was a psychologist named Dr Keith Hearne. Recently, I met up with Hearne at the Science Museum in London to see his original polygraph recordings and to hear first-hand his account of exactly what happened on that rainy spring morning in 1975 when he proved the impossible.

I started by asking Hearne to explain exactly how he set up the experiment – during which he needed to somehow send a signal from the lucid dream state to the sleep lab while the subject (a man named Alan Worsley) was still asleep and wired up to all the monitoring equipment.

'Well, you see,' he began, 'I'd tried micro switches on the subject's little finger, and all sorts of other things that we could use to communicate his awareness from within the dream, but none of them worked efficiently.

'And then I thought, *Ah! It's rapid eye movement sleep; the eyes aren't inhibited by the paralysis mechanism that affects the rest of the body, so perhaps he can communicate to me through the eyes?* I said to Worsley, "When you have a lucid dream, move your eyes left and right in consecutive motions as a way to communicate with me in the lab."'

'A kind of optical Morse code?' I said. 'Yes, if you like,' Hearne replied.

'So when did you first get the signals?' I asked.

'I almost missed it actually,' Hearne said. 'The previous week I'd had Worsley wired up for the whole night and each time he entered a REM period I would sit there, goggle-eyed, staring at the polygraph machine and watching the readouts. He went the whole night with no lucid dreams so at 8 a.m. I switched off all the equipment and started to pack up. Then, five minutes later, I heard him call from downstairs: "I just had a lucid dream, did you get it?" No! I'd missed it by five minutes! Thank God we repeated the test the next week though.'

'So a week later you did the same experiment?' I asked.

'Yes, that's when it all came together. It was just gone 8 a.m., and he was in a REM period when suddenly the eye movement signals came through, distinct patterns on the EOG (eye movement records) while he was still sound asleep.'

'So this guy was totally asleep, unconscious to the outside world and then suddenly he became conscious within his dream and was aware enough to think, *Okay, I'd better do the eye signals, to communicate with Keith in the lab*?' I asked.

'Yes, but in fact he was a bit annoyed that he had to make the signals because he was more interested in enjoying his lucid dream! I think I was much more aware that history was being made than he was.'

'What was it like when you first saw those eye signals come through?' I asked.

Hearne's own eyes lit up at this. 'It was fantastic! I was overwhelmed by it. It was like getting signals from another world, from another universe, even. In fact it happened on 12 April 1975 and interestingly it was on 12 April 1961 that NASA received the first messages from a man in space. I felt like those guys at NASA, except that I was receiving the first messages from *inner* space!'

Hearne's excitement turned to wistfulness for a moment as he said, 'But you know how you see the NASA control rooms in films and they all give each other high fives and congratulate each other? I had no one to high five! I had just scientifically proven lucid dreaming and I had no one to high five...'

'Oh no, give me a high five now, man!' I interjected. 'Forty years too late, but still...' We shared an awkward high five.

'I could have done with that 40 years ago, Charlie!' Hearne said. 'Thank you. You know, seeing these polygraph recordings makes me quite emotional actually, even now. To remember that we did it, we proved it, we proved the paradox...' He gestured to the original polygraph readings that were on display in a Perspex box behind us.

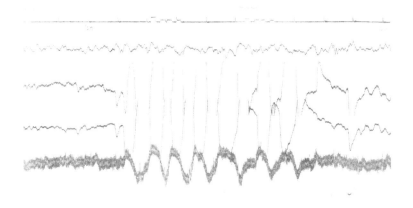

The first ever recorded ocular signals from a person in a lucid dream:
The two central bands above show the movement records for the left and right eyes. We can clearly see just how definite the eye movement signals were when compared to the jittery, short waves of rapid eye movement that both precede and follow them.

'And thank you for the high five, Charlie, I'm glad you did that. You can put that in your book, too.'

'So you got the results, but what happened next?' I continued.

'Well, I knew I'd discovered something big so I wrote to all the major sleep laboratories around the world – among them Chicago and Stanford – and then, after delivering my findings at a conference at Hull University, I moved to Liverpool to continue my studies.'

I then asked Hearne: 'As we approach the fortieth anniversary of your discovery, what do you think have been lucid dreaming's major contributions to the world?'

'It's a new form of recreation for one thing, and it doesn't cost you anything,' he replied. 'It shows people new ways of exploring reality and also it gives people freedom. You know, I've always felt sorry for people serving life terms in prison. The idea of keeping people locked up for life frightens me. I think lucid dreaming can help them to experience freedom – and it might help them to integrate regrets from their past too.'

Visit www.keithhearne.com to learn more about Dr Keith Hearne's work.

As we walked away, dodging the hordes of schoolchildren that thronged the Science Museum's corridors, I looked back at Dr Hearne and realized that he too might have some regrets from his past. You see, the story of his discovery is not so simple. As with many great stories, there's often another version.

The other version

Around the same time that Hearne was pioneering the scientific verification of lucid dreaming in the UK, a young American scientist called Stephen LaBerge was starting work on his PhD in psychophysiology in California. Working at Stanford University, LaBerge set out to prove the existence of lucid dreaming for what he thought was the first time in history.

Although Hearne delivered a paper to a conference on behavioural sciences in 1977, and then published his PhD thesis a year later, 'the scientific establishment resisted accepting his results'.[13] This meant that his findings were simply never widely circulated, peer-reviewed or disseminated across the Atlantic, so when LaBerge finally got similar results using similar methods, he naturally believed that he'd broken new ground.

Whether LaBerge knew about Hearne's results or not is seen by many as inconsequential nowadays, for LaBerge became the man who invented the techniques, wrote multiple books on the subject and became the poster boy for lucid dreaming across the globe. Also, it was LaBerge who first empirically demonstrated that it's possible to be self-aware in the REM sleep state[13] using EEG, whereas Hearne only demonstrated it was possible to signal awareness from the dream state.

So, although it's Hearne's ground-breaking research that we must revere, without LaBerge's tireless work over the last three decades, in both the public and scientific spheres, lucid dreaming might still be viewed as too 'woo woo' to be true. Personally, I think that both Hearne and LaBerge are brilliant men who stood on the shoulders of the giants who preceded them – and each saw as far as each other into a realm of possibility overlooked for so long.

Chapter 6

Lucid dreaming around the world – sangomas, shamans and lucid lamas

N ow that we've explored the West, let's take a look at a few of the rich lucid dreaming practices found in other parts of the world.

Dreaming on the roof of the world

At the end of my teens I formally became a Buddhist by taking refuge with a Tibetan Lama named Akong Rinpoche.[1] Once I'd started going on meditation retreats I began to hear people use the term 'dream yoga'. On one such occasion a monk was explaining how this is the name given to a series of dream, sleep and out-of-body experience practices found within Tibetan Buddhism that have lucidity training at their core.

The monk told me how dream yoga is used to practise meditation within the lucid dream, to train for the dying-and-death process, and even to gain insight into the very nature of waking reality. We spoke of meditating yogis entering the dream consciously and of lamas using the lucid dream state to eject their consciousness out into the pure realms. I was transfixed.

I began to devour books on the subject and learned how lucid dream training is used to prepare us for the 'after-death bardo[2] state' – the dreamlike hallucinatory experience that we enter into once our mindstream has separated from the body at the point of death. Apparently, if we can truly master lucid dreaming then at the point of death we can become lucid within the dreamlike 'after-death bardo', recognize the nature of mind and reach full spiritual enlightenment. Lucid dreaming within Tibetan Buddhism is taken very seriously.

So let's hear more about this subject from my teacher, a Tibetan dream yoga master named Lama Yeshe Rinpoche. I interviewed Rinpoche at Samye Ling Monastery in Scotland, where he lives as the Abbot, and began by asking him about the role dream yoga plays in Tibetan Buddhism.

'Dream yoga is an essential practice for our lineage,' he told me. 'Within our tradition we have something called the Six Yogas of Naropa, which is seen as one of the most profound sets of practices. One of these Six Yogas is dream yoga.

'In dream yoga we learn practices to help us recognize the dream and become lucid. Once we're lucid in the dream anything is possible, so we can learn to travel to different planets, we can manifest one thing into a thousand and a thousand things into oneness.'

I then asked him about the relationship between death and lucid dreaming.

'Death and dreaming, it's all the same, just different interpretations. Once we achieve stabilized lucidity in dreams, when death comes we can see the death bardo as a dream too. This leads to fearlessness of death because we know that we can recognize the death bardo and achieve full awakening.'

'Why do you think there's so much interest around lucid dreaming nowadays, Rinpoche?' I asked.

'The West is ready for these practices now because in these modern times everybody is so concerned with themselves – with the "I" – and this makes everything seem so solid and real. But in lucid dreaming the sense of "I" is less solid, less real.

'Because in the lucid dream you're everything; it's all mind?' I interjected.

'Yes! Of course! So lucid dreaming helps to free us from the solidification of "I". And if there's no "I" then there's no suffering, because there is no "I" to suffer. Lucid dreaming cushions us – it shows us the lack of self and acts like a safety net to help us practise for the dream everyday life.

'Through lucid dreaming we come to see that our everyday life is also like a dream, a longer dream but still a dream. There is no actual reality. If we can know this then our everyday life becomes far less solid and we see that the essence of everything is based on the pure nature of unconditional compassion – just like a dream.'

Visit www.samyeling.org for more information about Lama Yeshe Rinpoche and the Kagyu Samye Ling Monastery.

Strange but true

In some schools of Tibetan Buddhism it is advised to sleep sitting upright in meditation posture all night as a way to maintain lucid awareness throughout sleep. If that seems a bit extreme, then you might like to just try a higher pillow than usual as a way to help maintain clarity.

The Toltec-Mexihca tradition

Apart from Tibetan Buddhism, the other ancient dream lineage I've had the most personal experience of is the Toltec-Mexihca tradition. At the time of writing, I'm halfway through the Lucid Dreaming World Tour with my friend and teacher Sergio Magaña. Sergio is the author of *The Toltec Secret*, and in 2013 he was named the UNESCO representative for the preservation of the Toltec-Mexihca tradition.

I picked Sergio's brains about the origins of his dream-work tradition, and this is what he told me: 'There are two versions to explain where the dreaming practices in the Toltec-Mexihca tradition originated. The oral tradition says there was a group of dreamers named "the people of the halo of the moon" who lived in a place called Teotihuacan 50,000 years ago, and that they were the first dreamers. These people created two different lineages of what's called *nahualism*: the ancient dreaming knowledge of Mexico.'

'One of the lineages was that of the Mexihca (the people of the moon), who would use plants like the hallucinogenic peyote to open their awareness, along with specific shamanic formulas like ingesting the powdered body of a snake in order to invite the spirit of the serpent into dreams. The other lineage was that of the Toltec, who focused more on breath-work techniques based on the mathematics of the universe, and the use of ritual dances too. It's from these two lineages that the modern Toltec and Mexihca cultures of the past thousand years took their names.'

'And what about the other version?' I asked Sergio.

'The other version, and the more official one I should add, is that a nomadic group named the chichimecas, the "people of the double power", awake and sleeping, who lived in the USA and Mexico, began these practices about 4,000 years ago. These dreaming practices are almost extinct now, though. I've only found four people in the whole of Mexico who know deeply about them. This is because there was a command from the last Aztec ruler to hide the treasures – the Spanish thought this was gold, but actually it was knowledge of the dream practices. It was then prophesied that, with the dawning of the sixth sun, these treasures will return. The time of the sixth sun began in 2012, so now is the time to reveal these ancient practices once more.'

I asked Sergio how he'd first come into contact with these practices. 'My nanny was actually one of those four people who really knew about the dream practices. She was the daughter of a well-respected healer, or *curandero*, of an indigenous group called the *otomíes*. She had some knowledge and so that was my first meeting with the dreaming world. Then I found my teachers many years later.'

Sergio went on to explain some of the lucid dreaming techniques within his tradition. 'The main techniques are certain breathing exercises that we do before sleep in order to plant dreams and to encourage lucid dreaming. There are also some more sophisticated techniques like the *chac mool*, which involves breath work that actually changes your reflection while you gaze into an obsidian mirror.

'As you do this you can command how you would like to appear in the dream world, depending on what aspect of your life you want to work with: healing or abundance, for example, or whatever you wish.

'We also look for the spirit of the sun, moon, and stars in our dreams. Before this we would do a full-moon ceremony involving many dreamers in which the dreamers who become lucid can appear in each other's dreams.'

For more information on Sergio's work, visit www.sergiomagana.com or check out his new book, *The Toltec Secret.*

Shamanic lucidity

There's a great story about a journalist who was studying indigenous tribal cultures around the world. When he introduced himself as an American to the leaders of the various tribes, on three different occasions three different tribal leaders from three different corners of the world all asked him: 'You're an American? Do you know Stanley Krippner? He lived with us before.'

I had the honour of meeting the legendary octogenarian anthropologist at the Gateways of the Mind Conference in

2013 and have since had the chance to speak to him about shamanic lucid dream practices from around the world.

Dr Krippner began by telling me what shamans actually are: 'They are socially sanctioned practitioners who obtain information in ways not accessible to their peers. This information is used to heal or help their social group. Lucid dreaming is one source of this information.'

'So lucid dreaming plays a central role in some shamanic traditions, then?' I asked.

'One shaman I spoke to in Brazil told me that "anyone who dreams partakes in a bit of shamanism", although I don't know of any shamanic traditions where lucid dreaming plays a *central* role. But there are, of course, individual shamans who use lucid dreaming as a central focus. One of my students wrote her dissertation on a Native American medicine man called Rolling Thunder who was a "dreamwalker" with the ability to enter other people's dreams and offer them healing.

'And as you know, lucid dreaming is cultivated by many Tibetan lamas, and that tradition goes back to the Bon tradition, which grew out of shamanism.'

I asked Stanley why lucid dreaming was so important to some shamanic practitioners.

'Lucid dreaming was, and still is, important in these traditions because dreaming is felt to be a portal into other worlds. If one can control one's dreams, this portal can be accessed more directly. Also there are practical benefits: the shaman can dream about which herbs are needed to heal sick people or what rituals can be conducted to produce rain.'

'It seems as if the shamans use lucid dreaming in a much more practical way than is done in the West, where it's often used as a form of recreation,' I remarked.

'Oh yes, and many scholars of comparative religions make the point that Eastern practitioners of lucid dreaming use procedures that are far more complex and sophisticated than those recently adopted by Westerners too.'

Finally, I couldn't resist asking the man who'd been so instrumental in spreading awareness of plant medicine to the West whether the lucid dream experience could be compared to the plant-medicine experience of ayahuasca.

Also known as *yage*, ayahuasca is a blend of two plants – the ayahuasca vine (*Banisteriopsis caapi*) and a shrub called chacruna (*Psychotria viridis*), which contains the psychedelic compound dimethyltryptamine (DMT). It forms part of the ancient medicine lineages of the Amazonian region.

'Although some anthropologists speculate that the development of lucid dreaming is a cognitive development that may change the actual neurology of the dreamer – which can be seen to resemble initiation into ayahuasca use – the only direct connection between ayahuasca experiences and lucid dreaming is that many people claim to have lucid dreams immediately after their ayahuasca experience is over. But this is anecdotal. No studies have been done on this topic.'

Visit www.stanleykrippner.weebly.com for more information on Stanley Krippner's work.

Lucid Sufis and Islamic dream work

Sufism is a mystic aspect or dimension of Islam[3] that has strong threads of dream work and lucid dreaming running through it. The Spanish Sufi Ibn al-Arabi said that 'a person must learn to control his thoughts in a dream. The training of this alertness will produce great benefits for the individual.'[4] He also encouraged people to learn lucid dreaming by saying that 'everyone should apply himself to the attainment of this ability'.

I interviewed Nigel Hamilton, the UK representative of the Sufi Order International, about lucid dream practice within his tradition and he told me that 'although the Arabic Sufi orders talk about revelations being received through dreams it's the fact that these can lead to waking-state visions that is seen to hold the most potential'.

He added that 'due to the interaction between Sufis and the Indian yogis there are some lucid dream practices found in Sufism that came originally from the Indian Vedanta tradition. One of these involves meditation on a red dot in the third eye chakra, which seems to be similar to certain Tibetan Buddhist dream yoga techniques too.'

Since its formation over 1,400 years ago, the whole of Islam – not just Sufism – has had a close relationship with dreaming. The Prophet Muhammad himself used his dreams to advise on both military and religious matters, and much of the Koran was revealed to him through his dreams. There is even a line from the Koran that says that dream work is 'the prime science since the beginning of the world'.[5]

The Prophet would 'ask his disciples every morning about their dreams and offer interpretations of them'.[6] Interestingly, the famous Islamic call to prayer (*adhan*) was instituted by Muhammad after one of his close disciples dreamed of such a thing and shared the dream with him.

There's a framework of formalized dream practice in Islam, too, called 'Istikhara'. In this, specific prayers are recited during the day as a way of receiving a sought-after dream of guidance that night.[7]

The Xhosa of South Africa

I've known South African sangoma John Lockley for a few years now but recently I asked him to help elucidate the dream work practices of the Xhosa (pronounced K'ozza, with a click on the K if you're brave enough) tribe of South Africa, of which he is part.

John began by telling me how the Xhosa sangoma culture is an ancient oral tradition with teachings and practices passed on from one generation to the next.

'The Xhosa tribe is connected to the Khoisan (Bushmen) people, who are known to be the earliest inhabitants of southern Africa. They were hunter-gatherers who intermarried with the Xhosa people from the 1700s onwards, and it's thought that some of the dream practices that the Xhosa sangomas now work with came originally from the Khoisan people.'

I asked John how well known the Xhosa dream practices are these days. 'The practices are well known among Xhosa sangomas and their apprentices, as well as sangomas from other lineages,' he told me. 'I'm currently trying to help promote these indigenous dream practices around the world. However, it seems there is little awareness of these ways in the Western world at present.'

I continued by asking him how he'd got into indigenous African dream work, especially growing up as a white South African during the apartheid era.

'I had a dream when I was 18 years old in which I was called to become a traditional sangoma medicine man,' John replied. 'I was told in that dream that if I accepted the calling I was going to get very sick. This sickness is known as the "twaza", or "illness of calling", and it's very common among sangoma initiates.

'My "twaza" illness was really debilitating. I had fevers, night sweats, anxiety and depression. It led to a huge flush of electrical energy through me. In South Africa we call this flow of nervous energy "umbilini". It's similar to the concept of kundalini in the Indian traditions.'

'So what happened next?' I asked.

'Well, as a white man I wasn't allowed into the segregated black areas so I couldn't find my sangoma teacher. But my dreams soon guided me around this obstacle. They first showed me to Zen Buddhism and guided me to work with a Zen master out in South Korea. I then returned to South Africa in 1994, when Mandela became president and apartheid finally ended. I found my sangoma teacher a few years later and she confirmed my dream experiences and taught me the ways of her people.'

I asked John what those 'ways' were, exactly.

'Essentially there are three main practices that stimulate our dreams and help us gain clarity in our everyday lives. These are rhythm work, medicinal plants and ancestral prayers. The sangoma rhythm is a particular heartbeat rhythm and it's played on a large drum called an "isiguba". We dance to this rhythm.

'Then there's the use of medicinal plants, which are used to help cleanse the body both internally as drinks and externally as washes applied to the skin. Generally, non-hallucinogenic plants are used.

'And finally, prayer is of course essential to the path. Sangomas pray to their ancestors, guardian spirits and uThixo – the Great Spirit. They pray in a particular, rhythmical way, allowing the prayers to move up from their bones and blood. All this has a big effect on your dreams.'

Check out www.johnlockley-sangoma.com for more information about John's work around the world.

Inspired by those amazing lucid dream traditions? Then let's get back to the one tradition found within them all: doing the practices!

🧰 TOOLBOX 5: ACCESSING THE ICEBERG

Our toolboxes are filling up fast, so let's look now at a classic lucid dreaming technique found in many of the dream traditions we learned about in Chapter 6. This technique allows us to access the iceberg of the unconscious directly, without losing conscious awareness.

Falling Asleep Consciously

For many people falling asleep consciously, or FAC, is the Holy Grail of lucid dreaming practice, but it's really not such a big deal. Although it can take a long time to master it, I've taught hundreds of people this technique and seen them apply it successfully within a few weeks – or even on the first night of practice.

FAC combines elements of a well-known lucid dreaming technique called WILD (wake-initiated lucid dream) with a few of my own methods and a twist of meditative awareness. The aim is to pass through the hypnagogic state and enter REM dreaming sleep without blacking out or losing consciousness. FAC is both incredibly simple and often incredibly elusive, and involves letting your body and brain fall asleep while part of your mind stays aware.

I advise that you practise this technique after briefly waking in the last few hours of your sleep cycle, when you will enter REM dreaming straight from the hypnagogic state. As we learned in toolbox 2, when you first fall asleep it may be 80 minutes before you enter your first dream period but if you wake yourself in the early hours (either naturally or with an alarm) and then fall back asleep you'll enter dreaming within about 15 minutes. For this technique it's a case of the more direct the entry into the dream state the better.

I have three favourite versions of the FAC technique that I teach. Let's look at each one individually.

The FAC (falling asleep consciously) technique

Five steps to hypnagogic drop-in

To enter the dream state lucidly, be like a surfer. Paddle through the hypnagogic imagery and 'drop in' to the wave of the dream lucidly. If you have a good sense of mental balance and awareness then this is the technique for you!

1. After at least four and a half hours of sleep, wake yourself up and write down your dreams. Then set your intent to gain lucidity, close your eyes and allow yourself to drift back into sleep.

2. As you enter the hypnagogic state, gently focus your mental awareness on the hypnagogic imagery and simply float through it, allowing it to build, layer upon layer. The key here is to maintain a delicate vigilance without blacking out and being sucked into the dream state unconsciously.

3. Don't engage the hypnagogic imagery that'll arise, but don't reject it either. Just lie there watching it until the dreamscape has been formed sufficiently for you to drop into it consciously. If you feel yourself blacking out, just keep bringing your focus back to the hypnagogic imagery. It'll continue to build, layer upon layer, until it starts to coalesce into an actual dreamscape. This is a wonderful thing to witness.

4. As the dreamscape solidifies, you might feel a slight pull or a sensation of being sucked forwards. This is an indication that the wave of the dream is now fully formed. In surfing terms, you're on point break.

5. If you can just stay conscious for a few more moments, and are ready to take the plunge, you'll find yourself dropping into the wave of the dream with full lucidity.

Five steps to body and breath

If you have good body awareness (perhaps you like to dance, or do body work or yoga), you may find that this version of the FAC technique is the one for you. It involves scanning your awareness through your body as you drift into sleep and enter the dream lucidly.

1. Some time after at least four and a half hours of sleep, wake yourself up and write down your dreams. Set your intent to gain lucidity, close your eyes and allow yourself to drift back into sleep.

2. As you enter the hypnagogic, gently focus your mental awareness on the sensations in your body, and the breath flowing through it. The hypnagogic imagery will still arise, but rather than focusing on it, as in the hypnagogic drop-in technique, this time focus on the sensations in your body. If you feel yourself blacking out, just keep bringing your focus back to the sensations of the body and breath.

3. You might find that systematically scanning your awareness through the body works well for this. Alternatively, you might choose simply to allow bodily sensations to attract your attention as they arise. Becoming aware of the contact points of your body on the bed works well too.

4. At some point you may actually feel the body paralysis that accompanies REM sleep. There's no need to freak out if this happens, it simply means that you're on the doorway of the dream.

5. Once you've scanned your body, or allowed your attention to be aware of particular sensations, become aware of your whole body as it lies in space. Hold your entire body within your awareness and allow your mind to remain lucid as the dream forms out of the hypnagogic and you enter it lucidly

Five steps to counting sleep

This version of the technique isn't particularly meditative, and it doesn't call for much body awareness either, but it does require the ability to maintain a sense of reflective awareness as you abseil down into the dream. By combining counting with a repeated question (or reflection) as you go through the transition from wakefulness into dream, you can maintain your awareness fluidly.

1. Some time after at least four and a half hours of sleep, wake up fully and write down your dreams. Set your intent to gain lucidity, close your eyes and allow yourself to drift back into sleep.

2. As you enter the hypnagogic, continuously question your state of consciousness as you count yourself into dreaming. For example: *One: Am I dreaming? Two: Am I dreaming?* and so on. I prefer to use: *One: I'm lucid? Two: I'm lucid?* for this technique, but use whatever feels right for you.

3. For the first few minutes the answer to the question will probably be *No, I'm still awake!*, but once you've counted into the 20s, it'll probably be *I'm now in the hypnagogic state.*

4. If you can make it into the thirties or forties, or even fifties, without blacking out, the answer may become *Almost! The hypnagogic is starting to solidify!* Limit your count to double figures though – once you start getting above 100 you may have overshot your mark and be too awake by then.

5. The eventual aim is to answer the question 'Am I dreaming?' with something like *Sixty-one: Am I dreaming? Hang on...yes, I'm dreaming! I'm lucid!* as you find yourself fully conscious within the dream.

The multiple wake-ups technique

It's been noted in the Tibetan Buddhist tradition that if we fall asleep once a night and wake up once in the morning, we're only giving ourselves one opportunity to fall asleep consciously – one opportunity to recall our dreams and one opportunity to engage the lucid dreaming techniques. But if we wake ourselves up and fall back to sleep three times a night then we triple our potential success rate! This idea forms the basis of the multiple wake-ups technique.

The first four and a half hours of sleep are when we get most of our deep, restorative sleep, so we don't interrupt those, but the second few hours, as you'll remember, are when we start to have longer dream periods, with the last two hours of our sleep cycle being the prime time for dreaming.

And don't worry, if we time the wake-ups to coincide with our 90-minute sleep cycles, we won't feel any less rested the following day.

On the lucid dreaming retreats I run we usually do wake-ups at 3.30 a.m., 5 a.m., 6:30 a.m. and 8 a.m. after a 10:30 p.m. bedtime. It's like a nine-hour spiritual slumber party each night!

Here's how it's done. Set your alarm so that you wake up after at least four and a half hours sleep and then, once you've written down your dreams for five to ten minutes, reset your alarm for 90 minutes later and fall asleep practising your chosen lucid dreaming technique. Repeat as required.

Staying in the dream

Now that you have five toolboxes full of techniques to work with you're going to start having lucid dreams very soon (if you haven't already, that is) so let's turn our attention now to how to stay in the lucid dream state once we get there.

As I mentioned in Chapter 1, the most common form of lucid dream for newbie dreamers goes something like this: they're dreaming away, totally unaware that they're dreaming and then suddenly something weird happens and they think, *Hang on, this is a dream! I'm lucid dreaming! Oh my gosh! This is so...*

And they then find themselves instantly woken up by the sheer excitement of it all. Excitement and awe are two of my favourite emotions, but if we want to stay lucid for more than a few seconds we need to learn how to keep them in check. The man who taught me how to do this is one of the leading authorities on lucid dreaming – Robert Waggoner – so I thought it'd be great if he could teach you guys how to stay cool too.

Tips from the pros: Keep calm and carry on, with Robert Waggoner

You've done it! You've become lucidly aware. Incredibly, you stand (or float, or hover) in a dream, knowing it as a dream. It's an amazing feeling.

However, one important element may pull the plug on your lucid adventure, and quickly make it all disappear – *your emotions*. Almost every lucid dreamer learns that too much emotional intensity will pop you out of the lucid dream. So probably the first thing that you need to realize as soon as you become lucid is this: keep calm and carry on.

The amount of emotional intensity differs from lucid dreamer to lucid dreamer. You may find yourself able to deal with a surprising amount of joy, euphoria and glee before you trigger the lucid ejection button. At some point though, you will likely discover that limits exist to the amount of emotion you can feel in a lucid dream.

❖ What to do? It's really quite easy. At my workshops, I urge beginning lucid dreamers to monitor the level of emotions. If you seem too excited, then do one or more of the following practices:

❖ Mentally tell yourself to *calm down, chill, take it easy*. This simple suggestion can cause an immediate reduction in the level of emotion.

❖ Look away from anything that increases your emotions. If you lucidly see Brad Pitt and Angelina Jolie, don't let your emotions spike! Instead, look down at the ground or at your feet. Looking away from the exciting scene will often dramatically reduce your emotions. Of course, once you calm down, you can get their autograph, have a nice lucid dream chat and take them on a lucid flight around the dreamscape.

❖ Finally, you can look at your hands for a few seconds to reduce the amount of emotion, and centre your awareness. I learned this practice from Carlos Castaneda, in the book *Journey to Ixtlan*. Not only did looking at my hands help centre me, but it seemed to revive my focus and energy for more thoughtful lucid dreaming.

✦ So there you have it. Three practical techniques you can use to prolong your lucid dream when you realize that your emotions are reaching a critical stage. If you can't recall all three in your lucid dream, then just try to remember this very simple intent: 'keep calm and carry on'. With that in mind, you'll do fine.

Robert Waggoner is author of the acclaimed book *Lucid Dreaming: Gateway to the Inner Self* and co-editor of the magazine *Lucid Dreaming Experience*. He's a past president of the International Association for the Study of Dreams and conducts workshops around the world on his life's passion, lucid dreaming.

CHARLIE'S TOOLBOX CHECKLIST ✍️

✦ The FAC technique might take some time to master, so give yourself a good few nights with each variant of it before moving on to the next one.

✦ The hypnagogic drop-in technique is fundamentally about meditating into sleep so you might want to boost your chances of success by doing some mindfulness meditation exercises during the day.

✦ If you're going to do the multiple wake-ups technique be sure to set your alarm as you proceed through the night, so that you can maintain the exact 90-minute periods between each session.

✦ Your alarm is going to become a feature of your night-time activity if you want to do these practices so try and get hold of a soothing alarm sound that'll wake you up softly and slowly.

❖ Don't forget to keep up the dream diary and reality checking during the daytime, as well as making a schedule for which night-time techniques to do on specific nights.

Chapter 7
Eating yourself lucid

We've looked at more than a dozen lucid dreaming techniques so far, but let's now take some time to explore how nature's best can bless our dream practice.

Dream vitamins, minerals and foodstuffs

There are plenty of artificial chemicals and pills that claim to give you lucid dreams, but nothing beats the practice of effective techniques. Having said that, there are quite a few vitamins and minerals that have been scientifically verified to make your dreams more vivid, while also contributing to your overall health.

The vitamin with the strongest effect on our dreams seems to be vitamin B6. A study from New York City College in the USA revealed 'a significant difference in dream vividness, bizarreness, emotionality, and colour between those given vitamin B6 and those given a placebo'[1] The study subjects were given 250mg of B6, which is quite a hit, so I'd recommend a smaller, 100-mg dose with a pre-bed snack for most people.

How does vitamin B6 work?

B6 converts amino acids such as tryptophan into serotonin, which leads to cortical arousal during periods of REM dreaming sleep.[2] It's this arousal of the brain which makes the dreams more vivid. B6 has also been linked to improved memory so it seems that this magic vitamin may help you remember those vivid dreams better too.

A range of other B vitamins, such as choline and B5, have also been linked to more vivid dreams, due to their role in making the REM neurotransmitter called acetylcholine, so a general vitamin B complex with a good dose of B6 should do the trick. Taking B6 supplements in excess of 1,000 mg/day can have adverse effects, though, so go easy.

Do I have to take it as a supplement?

No – if you can get it from food sources, all the better. Whole grains, liver and meat, eggs, beans, nuts and bananas all contain vitamin B6. Healthy adults need just 1.3mg of vitamin B6 each day for normal functioning and this can be achieved through a balanced diet. Although some researchers believe that you need to take a supplement to get enough B6 to affect your dreams significantly, they obviously haven't tried one of my B-vitamin bonanza super-green shakes. Check the references for my personal recipe.[3]

Dream expert Rebecca Turner advises a middle path. She recommends eating foods containing tryptophan (the amino acid converted by B6) around the same time you take your B6 supplement, a few hours before bed. Three of the most tryptophan-rich foods are chicken and turkey, soybeans and hard cheese. So there really is something to be said about cheese and dreams.

Calcium and magnesium

For many people, restful sleep and bountiful dreaming can be as simple as altering their diet to include calcium- and magnesium-rich foods. Studies have shown that a deficiency in these minerals may lead to an inability to enter sleep smoothly and to stay asleep once there.

Calcium

A study published in the *European Neurology Journal* reported that disturbances in sleep, especially the absence of REM and deep sleep, are often related to a calcium deficiency.[4] Calcium helps the brain use tryptophan to manufacture the sleep-inducing substance melatonin and so the more calcium we have the more melatonin we can produce. So the traditional milk-before-bedtime seems to hold some weight – or at least it did, because although the calcium levels in unpasteurized milk are high, once the modern heat treatment of milk takes place much of this is lost.

The *International Osteoporosis Foundation* cites sardines and whitebait as two of the foods with the highest calcium levels, along with almonds, sesame seeds and hard cheeses like parmesan and cheddar.[5]

Magnesium

This mineral plays an important role in hydration, muscle relaxation, energy production and, crucially, the deactivation of adrenaline. Magnesium is vital for the function of certain brain receptors which need to switch off before sleep, and without this process occurring we may remain tense, our thoughts racing as we lie in bed staring at the ceiling.[6] Research has shown magnesium can change people's sleep patterns within days, and I use it regularly myself to unwind my body and mind when I've been training in martial arts till late in the evening.

Many people, be they meat-eaters or vegetarians, are short of magnesium simply because it's found in such tiny doses in most foods nowadays, but if you eat enough dark leafy veggies, nuts and seeds (especially pumpkin seeds) and oily fish you'll soon get your daily dose.

Those who prefer to take a supplement can often find magnesium and B vitamins in a combined tablet, which can be taken with a pre-bed snack. People with digestive issues may not absorb minerals so well and may instead prefer magnesium sprays, which are absorbed through the skin, or bathing in magnesium salts before bed.

Note: All of the vitamins and minerals mentioned above are safe in the correct doses, and are great for giving you more vivid dreams, but please be careful about getting into the habit of popping a pill to aid your lucid dream practice.

Eat like a northerner

My fiancée is from Yorkshire in the north of England, and in honour of the cultural heritage of that region she likes to call her midday meal 'dinner' and to eat her evening meal at 5 p.m. As a Londoner, I find this far too early to eat in the evening, but it does have one big advantage. Eating early is great for your dream practice.

The earlier you eat the easier it is for the body to be rested by the time you go to bed. If you drift off while your gut is still working on digesting your food, your body will be diverting energy to the gut that should be going to your brain to help power your dreams.

During the lucid dream retreats I run we just have soup and salad at 6 p.m., as a way to free up our bodies for the night of dreaming that lies ahead. Tibetan Buddhist monks and nuns often don't eat anything after midday, or if they do eat in the evening it's usually something very light because from a Tibetan Buddhist point of view going to sleep on an empty stomach allows the internal energy to flow more freely through the subtle channels, which is seen as an aid to dream practice.

Don't drink and dream

Although there are B vitamins in a pint of Guinness, alcohol is a big obstacle to dream practice. Booze is a depressant, so it zonks you out, makes you less likely to be bothered to do any lucid dreaming practice and sometimes makes you act like an idiot.

According to the National Institute of Neurological Disorders and Stroke in the USA, although it may feel as if you're sleeping very deeply if you go to bed drunk, in fact 'alcohol only helps people fall into light sleep, and it also robs them of REM and the deeper, more restorative stages of sleep'.

Cannabis is another drug that really messes with your dream periods and makes dreams harder to recall – and I speak from youthful experience. A weed habit is incompatible with a lucid dreaming practice.

Sniffing out lucidity

Have you ever smelled a certain scent that instantly conjures up vivid memories of the past? Imagine if that memory could be used as a dream sign. Scent association is a lucid dreaming technique that was first documented by the nineteenth-century lucid dreaming pioneer the Marquis d'Hervey de Saint Denys.

The French nobleman wore a particular perfume every day during a visit to mountains in southern France and then stopped wearing it once he returned home. A few months later he told his servant to sprinkle a few drops of the perfume on his pillow on random nights while he slept. On those nights he found that he would dream of the mountains, this would act as a dream sign (because he was no longer in the mountains) and help him become lucid.

If you want to try a similar experiment, or simply want some help with your dream recall, I'd advise using the scent of rosemary because inhaling micro particles of this herb has been scientifically proven to help boost memory by inhibiting the enzymes which block normal brain functioning.[7]

But what about other scents that will send us to the land of lucidity?

Mugwort

Called *nagadamni* in Sanskrit, mugwort has been used in Ayurveda medicine for hundreds of years to treat cardiac conditions, as well as feelings of unease, anxiety and general malaise. It's been employed for ages as a reliable dream-enhancing plant by many shamanic practitioners, who know that smudging with it (wafting the smoke around the body and allowing some to be inhaled too) before bed can lead to a marked increase in dream vividness and recall.

NB: Pregnant women should avoid prolonged exposure to mugwort.

Clary sage

This herb is often used in aromatherapy for relieving anxiety and fear, menstrual-related problems and insomnia. It's also great for bringing on more vivid dreams. Although it doesn't smell that nice I found that sprinkling a few drops of the oil onto a tissue and inhaling them as I fell asleep brought on intensely vivid dreams each night I used it.

NB: It's best not to use clary sage if you've been drinking alcohol, as apparently this can lead to nightmares.[8]

Strange but true

Scary smells can lead to scary dreams. German researchers discovered that smells in your bedroom can significantly affect your dreams. They used specific smells with negative or positive connotations (such as rotten eggs or roses) to affect subjects during sleep. They discovered, unsurprisingly, that unpleasant smells often led to unpleasant dreams while rose-scented bedrooms led to rose-tinted dreams.[9]

Camalonga seed essence

At a Gateways of the Mind conference I met a woman called Mimi who told me that she was a shaman who'd spent seven years in the Amazon. She wanted me to try a new dream-enhancing essence that she'd made from the seeds of the camalonga tree – a teacher plant that works in the dream time to stimulate lucid and vivid dreaming.

I asked Mimi to tell me more about the essence and she said that traditionally, male and female camalonga seeds are macerated in sugar-cane alcohol by the shaman, along with male and female camphor. The brew is then ingested before bed. The camalonga spirits work on straightening a person's energy while they're dreaming, thus leading to lucid dreams. Mimi told me that the spirit energy of the plant is in the essence, and that it is this that affects the dreams.

I thought this all sounded great, but when I discovered that this essence was just a mix of brandy and water containing none of the active compounds found in the camalonga seeds – merely their 'spirit' – I was ready to forget the whole thing. And I did for a couple of weeks. Then one night I thought I'd give it a shot. After joking with my fiancée that the six drops of brandy water would at least help me fall asleep quickly I soon drifted off through a non-eventful hypnagogic state.

And then the dreams came...

I had some of the biggest, most powerful lucid dreams, nightmares and false awakenings that I'd had in a long time! In the four nights I used the camalonga seed essence I had six long, lucid dreams and several big 'clarity' dreams of archetypal significance. After a break of a few days, during which time I had suitably normal dreams, I started taking it again and the rash of lucid energy that had entered my dreams previously came once again. This stuff worked. It seemed like the spirit of the camalonga seeds really was in the essence and it took my scepticism as a perfect opportunity to show its true power.

Visit www.sacredtreeessences.com for more information on Mimi's infusions.

Using the moon

Many Buddhists love full moons, and there are always special practices to be done on full-moon days. Why such love for a fat moon? Well, pretty much every important event in the historical Buddha's life is said to have happened on a full-moon day: his birth, his enlightenment and even his death.

Consequently it's said that the power of our meditation practice is amplified on full-moon days (and nights), and so we find various practices that are done especially at this time. In fact, at some Tibetan Buddhist centres there are even all-night compassion meditations that are done from 6 p.m. till 6 a.m. over the night of the full moon.

In ancient Indian tradition it's believed that the moon is the controller of the water, and it's said that the moon, like the other planets, exerts a considerable degree of influence over human beings. But do these beliefs have any science to back them up? Although most modern scientific studies exploring the moon's effects have negated this there are a couple that have found some interesting correlations.

A 2013 study published in the journal *Current Biology* proved that full moons really do affect our sleep. The research revealed that subjects took five minutes longer to fall asleep on the three or four nights surrounding a full moon and that, on average, they slept for 20 fewer minutes. In addition, EEG activity related to deep sleep fell by 30 per cent, and levels of the sleep hormone melatonin were lower.[10]

Much of this is great news for our lucid dreaming, because by falling asleep more slowly we float through the hypnagogic for longer and the decreased time we spend in deep sleep may mean more access to REM dreaming periods. If we combine these findings with the Buddhist view of spiritual practice being amplified through full moons, then we can see that scheduling a night of lucid dreaming on a full moon is a great idea!

Strange but true

Although there's no scientific backing to the long-held belief that changes in the moon can lead to a higher incidence of mental health issues, a study referred to in *Time* magazine concluded that there's a lunar link to the electrochemistry in the brain of epileptic patients, which changes in the few days surrounding a new moon, making seizures more likely.[11]

But enough about the moon, let's get back to learning how to shine bright at night with our final toolbox of techniques.

🧰 TOOLBOX 6: NOW THAT YOU'RE LUCID

We now have five toolboxes full of techniques to help us have lucid dreams, so let's have a look at what to *do* in those lucid dreams once we have them. Once lucid you can do pretty much anything you want to (as long as your unconscious agrees to let you do it, that is), but rather than just having sex with movie stars and flying about let's spend some time planning for a more beneficial lucid dream experience.

Lucid dream planning

Planning a lucid dream is a lucidity technique in itself, because when we set a strong intention to do something in our next lucid dream, we not only start to attract the causes and conditions needed to make that dream manifest, but we also create an expectation of becoming lucid.

On my workshops I teach three main stages to lucid dream planning: writing a dream plan, drawing a dream plan (the dreaming mind works in images, so this helps) and creating a *sankalpa* (a Sanskrit term which means 'will or purpose') – or statement of intent. But before we get to that, let me check through my personal dream diary to tell you about some of the things that I've been doing in my lucid dreams recently which might help to inspire your dream plans.

◆ Calling out in the dream to meet a personification of my inner child, then hugging him once he appeared and telling him that I love him.

- Turning everything in the lucid dream red as a way to experience a 'red dream'. Within the Toltec-Mexihca dream tradition it's believed that, due to red light being the light that filters through a mother's skin to her unborn baby, having a red dream is an experience of healing and rebirth.

- Meditating within the lucid dream and manifesting a huge Amitabha Buddha (the Buddha of infinite light) in the sky before me, while reciting the Amitabha prayer.

- Exploring how the perception of time can be transformed once lucid by intentionally slowing down and speeding up certain parts of the dreamscape at will.

- Self-inception of the affirmation 'I am happy, healthy and helpful in every single way, I am happy, healthy and helpful every single day' by calling it out within the lucid dream.

- Asking the lucid dream: 'What is the essence of kindness and compassion?' and then being swept from the dream into an infinite void in which I was told that 'the universe loves every being always and you are loved by the universe. This is the essence of kindness.'

- Healing my shortsightedness through a combination of hands-on healing within the lucid dream and calling out: 'There is no conflict in the muscles of my eyes! My eyes are healed!'

Feel free to try out any of these dream plans yourself, or, even better, why not create your own personal ones? Let me tell you how.

Five steps to lucid dream planning

1. Draft some ideas of what you'd like to do in your next lucid dream. What question would you like to ask? What activity would you like to engage in? What part of your psyche would you like to interact with?

2. Once you've decided what you want to do, begin to formulate your dream plan. Start with 'In my next lucid dream I...' and then write a description of what you want to do once lucid.

3. Next, draw a little picture of your dream plan in action. I just use stick men and speech bubbles when I draw my dream plans, but if you're artistic then of course feel free to do more.

4. Now write your *sankalpa*, or statement of intent. This should be a pithy statement that sums up the essence of your dream plan. For example, if your dream plan is a complex description of how you want to meet your inner child and embrace it with loving kindness, your *sankalpa* might be the much more concise 'inner child come to me!' Your dream plan can be as long and detailed as you like, but I recommend that you keep your *sankalpa* short and sharp.

5. The final step occurs when you next find yourself in a lucid dream. Once you get lucid, recall your dream plan, call your *sankalpa* out loud and then carry out your chosen dream plan.

The lucidity tank

I once asked my teacher Lama Yeshe Rinpoche why I'd sometimes become lucid without much effort and at other times it felt as if it was a real struggle. He replied in his broken Tibetan-English: 'Like an airplane, we need full tank of fuel to fly high. Same with lucid dreams. We need full tank.'

A full tank of what, though? A full tank of lucidity.

As lucid dreamers our job is to work out what fills up our lucidity tank and what depletes it. The level of our lucidity tank is not measured by our physical energy levels (although it's true that being too fatigued at bedtime can make lucid dreaming more difficult) but by our chi levels. Chi is a Chinese word for 'life force' – a bit like the concept of prana (internal wind energy) in Buddhism – and it's often our level of chi energy that determines how easy it will be to become lucid.

We can most readily raise our chi levels by engaging in energy work like chi gong, yoga or some energy-based martial arts, but we can also raise them by being creative, boosting our body awareness through dance or play and even by raising our oxytocin levels through laughter and acts of kindness.

Everybody's lucidity tank will be filled up and depleted in a totally unique way, so start to become aware of the way your own lucidity tank operates. For me personally, dance, meditation and energy work, kindness and laughter are all surefire ways to boost my lucidity levels, during both day and night. In fact I've even been known to watch 10 minutes of laugh-out-loud YouTube videos before bedtime as a way to fill up my lucidity tank before sleep!

Conversely I've found that reading work emails before bedtime, watching mindless TV and reading tabloid media are like putting a hole in my lucidity tank and leaking out all my chi energy.

So let's find out what fills up *your* lucidity tank.

Five steps to filling your lucidity tank

1. Draw an outline of your lucidity tank on a piece of paper. It can look however you want it to, but mine often resembles an oil drum or a fuel tank.

2. Have a think about what kind of things make you feel more aware, more energized and more lucid in the waking state.

3. On the *inside* of the tank, write or draw all the things that stock up your lucidity levels.

4. Now consider what kind of things make you feel *less* lucid, less aware and less energized. Then, on the *outside* of the tank, write down all these things that deplete your lucidity levels. You can even draw little arrows going from them, piercing the tank and leaking out the chi energy. Be creative – you can't get this wrong.

5. Finally, make a commitment to do more of what stocks up your lucidity tank and to do less of what depletes it! Keep your picture by your bed or in your dream diary as a reminder of the practice.

Enhancing your lucid dreaming practice

I want to end our final toolbox with a look at where we can take our practice from here – how we can further our lucidity training and what more we can do to develop our skills.

Learn to meditate

So many lucid dream techniques are dependent on holding our mind in check and maintaining our awareness so, if you're serious about lucid dreaming, it makes sense to learn meditation. I would personally recommend mindfulness meditation in particular if you want to develop a stabilized lucid dreaming practice. Mindfulness can be practised by people of all faiths and is based on the simple aspiration to 'know what's happening, as it is happening, without judgement or preference'.

Lucid dreaming isn't just analogous to mindfulness meditation, it *is* mindfulness meditation – 'knowing that we're dreaming as we're dreaming' (hopefully without judgement) – so it's the perfect practice for lucid dreamers. I recommend the Mindfulness Association (www.mindfulnessassociation.net) for courses around the UK and Europe, or, for courses in the USA, try Jon Kabat-Zinn's organisation www.umassmed.edu/cfm

Nap like a cat

Napping is one of the most beneficial things that you can do for both your psychological and physiological health. It charges your body with potential, and whatever activities you engage in after a nap will be executed more easily and tackled more creatively. It's also great for lucid dreaming! During an afternoon nap, we tend to enter REM dreaming sleep straight away and to stay there for most of the nap without much entry into delta-wave deep sleep, which means we get direct access to the dream state. To get the greatest benefits, nap for between 20 and 60 minutes.

Keep learning

This is an introductory book which simply lays the foundations of your lucid dream training but there are loads more techniques to explore and dozens of other great books out there to help further your learning, so get reading! Robert Waggoner's book *Lucid Dreaming: Gateway to the Inner Self* is my personal favourite, and then of course there is my own *Dreams of Awakening*, for those of you who are interested in using lucid dream training on the spiritual path.

Explore the hypnopompic

As a hypnopompic enthusiast it pains me that we've not had space within this book to fully explore this amazing state of consciousness, but let me at least plant the seed. As I touched on earlier, the hypnopompic state is the transitional state of mind that lies between sleep and full wakefulness. It's the state that we experience just before our mind has woken fully from sleep and when our eyes are still usually closed.

It's characterized by a soft clarity of mind, so you might like to hang out there if you can, resting in what's one of the most refined levels of consciousness. To do this, either wake yourself up slowly and gradually while keeping your eyes closed or hit the snooze button on the alarm and allow yourself to rest in the broad, panoramic awareness that characterizes the hypnopompic for an extra 10 minutes or so.

The hypnopompic can be a great place to access the lucid dream state too, by allowing yourself to slip back into the dream state through the back door. This is a favourite technique of my fiancée, Jade, who rests in the hypnopompic each morning while I'm clattering around the bedroom. In one of the lulls in my noisy activity she can allow herself to slip back into a dream with full lucidity. Give it a try yourself.

Make a schedule

Just as you'd schedule in your weekly exercise training, be sure to do the same with your lucidity training. Dream diaries and the Weird technique need to be done every day, but doing wake, back to bed every morning or having three alarms set to practise multiple wake-ups each night simply isn't practical for most people.

So the best thing to do is to schedule in at least one night a week for your lucid dream training, preferably on a night when you don't have to wake up too early the next morning. Choose the techniques you're going to practise, and when, and then stick to the schedule with discipline.

Have fun

Schedule and discipline are great but the easiest way to *stop* having lucid dreams is to get too uptight and rigid about the practice. Some people get so worried about having or not having lucid dreams that they can't even get to sleep from thinking about it. Of course we do need to make sure that we're doing the practices properly, but at the same time try and keep a sense of light-heartedness around the whole thing. And don't forget to have fun!

CHARLIE'S TOOLBOX CHECKLIST ✍

❖ Be sure to plan what you want to do in your next lucid dream, and feel free to have more than one dream plan to choose from. Remember that, once lucid, our ability to direct the dream is as much about our belief that anything is possible as it is about our level of friendship with the unconscious mind, so remind yourself that your dream plans are as achievable as you believe them to be.

❖ Be mindful of what stocks up and what depletes your lucidity tank. This will change over time, of course, so don't stop exploring.

❖ Try not to get disheartened if you don't start having lucid dreams straight away. Although some people have them within days of trying the techniques, most people take weeks to start seeing results, and months to have any stability in their practice. Lucid dreaming isn't easy, but then nothing worth learning ever is, so stick with it.

❖ Don't think that your journey ends once you've read this book – keep learning, keep exploring, and keep moving forward into lucidity!

Chapter 8
Healing, dreams of
the dead and lucid living

As this is the final chapter I feel that we're ready to venture deep into the ocean of wonder and weirdness that surrounds lucid dreaming. But let's start by dipping our toes into the incredible – but very real – potential of lucid dream healing.

We learned earlier that we can use lucid dreaming to work with nightmarish mental trauma, but now let's see how we can use it to work with *physical* trauma too. Just as we can use the 'total visualization' of the lucid dream state to heal our minds, let's now explore how we can use it to heal our bodies. There's growing evidence (both scientific and anecdotal) to suggest that once we become lucid we can engage physical healing responses while we sleep.

Lucid dream healing

Thousands of people have been helped in their recovery from illness by various types of waking-state visualized healing. One such method involves patients imagining their body's immune system manifesting in the form of coloured light, which can then heal their diseased cells.

A 2008 study published in the *Journal for the Society of Integrative Oncology* demonstrated how this type of visualized healing can even help reduce the risk of recurrence of breast cancer. Several other studies have shown that visualized healing can help to reduce stress, enhance the immune system's effectiveness and lessen pain in many patients.[1] However, many of these techniques are limited in that they're dependent on our ability to visualize – which will vary from person to person.

Lucid dreaming solves this problem because a lucid dream is the most vivid and complete visualization we may ever experience. This means that engaging visualized healing methods within the lucid dream may prove far more effective than in the waking state. The teachings of Tibetan Buddhism agree with this point too, as it's believed that visualizing in a lucid dream is 'far more powerful than simply visualizing in the waking state'.[2]

The esteemed dream researcher Jayne Gackenbach, from Virginia University in the USA, cites examples of lucid dream healing of everything from nicotine addiction and hives to weight loss. There's an overwhelming body of evidence in Robert Waggoner's book *Lucid Dreaming: Gateway to the Inner Self* to corroborate the potential of lucid dream healing too, and Toltec-Mexihca teacher Sergio Magaña has seen his students cure themselves of thyroid disease and nerve damage through lucid dream healing.

Personally, I've healed everything from addictive behaviour patterns to ear infections through lucid dreaming and have recently even been able to treat my shortsightedness through similar means. I haven't worn my glasses for over nine months now.

So how do we heal ourselves once we're lucid? If you wanted to heal your ear, for example, then once lucid you could apply hands-on healing within the lucid dream (often, white light will flow out of your hands at this point) and call out statements of healing intent such as, 'My ear is healed, my immune system is boosted!'

If you wanted to send healing to another person, you could simply call out statements of healing intent for them while lucid: 'May Diana be happy and well! May Diana be free from disease!', or perhaps even call forth a projection of the person into your dream and then apply hands-on healing directly.

One man believes in the power of lucid dream healing more than most, in part because it helped to cure him of kidney disease.

Case study: Healing kidney disease

Dreamer: *Bruno, Argentina*

Age: *32*

The lowdown from Bruno: *'In late 2011 doctors found I had a kidney disease called chronic renal failure. The diagnosis was that I had to receive a kidney transplant or otherwise I'd need dialysis within a few years. Due* *to the illness I started to meditate, and through that I discovered lucid dreaming. I can't say I'm sure that it was* only *this particular lucid dream that modified the deterioration of my kidneys but it did play a major role. I think the healing was also due to the many insights I received through meditation – I needed to change my perspective towards my kidneys – but then those meditations led me to learn lucid dreaming, so it's all connected, I guess.*

'When I began to practise lucid dreaming it helped me to appreciate that the self was not as real as I thought it was, and so I realized that the story *of me and my illness was unreal too. Letting go of the "poor me" story helped me to release the power of the disease too.'*

Bruno's dream report: *'It was a short dream, actually. I was walking through an ancient hall of marble and suddenly I became lucid. I felt something hit me from behind and fall to the floor. Instantly I recalled my dream plan: heal my kidneys.*

'Once I was lucid I placed both my hands behind my back, over the area of my kidneys, and I started to radiate healing energy specifically to them. Then I felt what seemed like an electric current moving out of my hand and reaching into my back and kidneys. It felt like a kind of tickling sensation. This lasted about 10 seconds. Then I woke up.'

Life after the dream: *'The whole process lasted more than a year but I can tell you that after that lucid dream, my kidneys stopped deteriorating and my* *creatinine level remained around 6.5 – which is stable – for nine months.*

'After the lucid dream I had an insight too: I realized that I don't have to ask for the kidneys to heal; instead I need to thank them for how well they have worked so far. So I started sending them the energy of "thanks for keeping me alive all this time", rather than "please heal now that you're diseased".

'I think it was the sum of many things which made the kidneys stop deteriorating; it all started with the reconciliation with my kidneys and my situation, but the lucid dream was the last, vital step.'

Bruno's experience is inspiring, not only because it's such a practical example of lucid dream healing but also because he saw that the lucid dream was only part of the process and that a new perspective of 'lucid living', which both his meditation and lucid dream training led to, played just as vital a role in the healing process.

At present we've barely scratched the surface of the full potential of lucid dream healing, but with future research, and the growing popularity of the subject, I believe that within a few years we may be able to apply it to a much wider range of ailments and perhaps use it as part of the treatment of some of the more serious conditions.

The other 1 per cent

Remember the ocean of weirdness that I promised we'd plunge into? One of the weirdest waves within this ocean of intrigue is something I like to call 'the other 1 per cent'.

I'm not talking about the elite 1 per cent of society here, but rather the elite 1 per cent of your dream which may well be made of something other than you.

I'm a firm believer that the vast majority of everything in our lucid dreams is made up of a projection of our own minds. A reductionist view of this would be that because scientists can now tell us what we're dreaming about from looking at our brain activity[3] (yup, its true, check the references section for more information), the brain plays a part in creating our dreams, meaning that dreaming, and lucid dreaming too, are at least in some part a product of our brain.

Although I believe that the brain is far more a receiver of consciousness rather than a creator of it, I do believe that dreams are predominantly products of our individual psyche. However, there's a small but crucial portion of our lucid dream experience – maybe 1 per cent, maybe more like 10 per cent, for those who know how to invite it in – that seems to come from something beyond our personal mindstream.

So what makes up this 1 per cent?

From the thousands of dream reports that I've heard, Tibetan Buddhist sources and my own research, it seems that the 1 per cent is primarily made up of universally existing archetypes of the collective unconscious, and from the universal mind which lies beyond that.

As well as this, the 1 per cent can also be made up of the energy, or at least the energetic imprint, of dead relatives to whom we had a strong connection. I know this all sounds pretty far out, but please just do a reality check and bear with me.

Although the vast majority of dead relatives who we meet in our lucid dreams are simply projections of our mind sourced from our memory, this is not the case 100% of the time.

The Buddhist meditation teacher Rob Nairn once speculated that our ancestors may leave a 'shroud of habitual patterns that survives after death' – an echo of their energy with which we can sometimes communicate after they've died. Communication with the energetic resonance of a dead relative can be difficult from the convincing solidity of the waking state, but if we can enter the more refined and flexible mental space of the lucid dream then it may be much easier.

In fact it seems that once we're lucid, on rare occasions we can often become a kind of 'light in the darkness' to which a recently dead relative might be attracted as they struggle to comprehend their after-death experience. If you do receive contact from a dead relative in a lucid dream then it's just as important to assure them that they are dead as it is to tell them that they are loved. Until they can accept that they are dead they may not be able to move fully through the after-death process. And even if who you are meeting in the lucid dream is just a projection of your own mind, then it's still important to say that, too, as a way to allow your own mind to let go of its grief and attachment.

Another slightly less spooky aspect of the 1 per cent is that which is made up of spiritually awakened individuals.

It seems that a side effect of full spiritual enlightenment is the capacity to enter other people's dreams. But how about the rest of us? Is it possible for everyday, 'non-fully enlightened' people to enter your lucid dreams too? Yes, but only if you've set your intention to let them in. Your lucid dreaming mind is heavily encrypted, much more so than your waking mind in my opinion, so don't worry about negative entities entering, because the enlightened energy required to be able to enter another's dream without their knowledge negates the potential of them getting in anyway.

How will I know the 1 per cent when I see it?

You won't need to ask. If you experience an aspect of the 1 per cent while you're lucid you'll know about it. They'll feel inherently different to everything else in the dream and have a presence that's tangibly dissimilar to all the other dream characters.

If a hologram suddenly popped up in front of you now, however realistic-looking it was you'd be able to tell me that it was a hologram, right? How? Because the energy of a hologram is tangibly different to that of a living being. So it is with the 1 per cent in our dreams.

One of my first experiences of the 1 per cent was after a period of misguidedly trying to enslave my unconscious. When I first started teaching lucid dreaming I felt totally out of my depth, I was only 25 years old and I felt as if things were happening much quicker than I'd planned. As a way to compensate for this lack of control I started to assert as much control as I could over my lucid dreams.

One of my favourite tricks was to yell out 'Stop!' and to watch the entire lucid dream freeze before me, *Matrix* style. I would then walk around the dream characters as they were frozen in place and look up at the dream birds, frozen in the sky. I could feel that this put the unconscious under huge tension, but I continued regardless.

One night I was in the middle of a lucid dream, about to yell 'Freeze!', when out of nowhere an old Tibetan woman walked into the dream and tapped me on the shoulder. She felt different to anything I'd ever encountered previously in the lucid dream state. She looked at me and said: 'Stop controlling your dreams. We don't like it.' It was me who then froze. I stood in shock as I asked myself, *Who the hell is WE*?

It seems that the Tibetan woman who entered my lucid dream may have been part of that 1 per cent: a universally existing archetype (the wise woman) of the collective unconscious who'd kindly come to show me the error of my ways. Who the mysterious 'we' was that she referred to I still don't know.

Let's look now at a fine example of not only the 1 per cent but of how lucid dreaming can be used as a tool for self-reflection and letting go of judgement.

Case study: Letting go

Dreamer: *Millie, UK*

Age: *32*

The lowdown from Millie: *'My dad died when I was 12 and ever since I learned about lucid dreaming I* *wondered if it would be possible to meet him in a lucid dream. I couldn't stop thinking about how amazing it would be to do that now I'm an adult. I wanted to see if he knew about what goes on in our lives and if he approved of it all. I think the approval thing was especially important for me.'*

Millie's dream report: *'I was just having a normal dream and then I started flying in it. Flying is my dream sign so I knew to do a reality check. I looked at my hand and flipped it over. It went all funny-looking and I became lucid.*

'There was a gap in the sky and I knew that through it was some sort of deeper level of lucid dream, or even maybe a portal to something beyond. It was brighter and I knew that I had to get to it. Then, BAM! I broke through into this new dream space and it was so bright and colourful.

'Instantly I knew that now was the time to ask to see my dad. Next thing I knew there he was, just standing there with my dog Pip, who passed away years ago too. They were standing outside the community hall near our house, but it all looked a bit different. So there he was, my dad. But it wasn't like a projection of my dad, or like he was part of the lucid dream, it was as if it was actually my dad. When I saw him we hugged and it felt so real!

'The first thing I said was, "Dad! You look exactly the same!" The lucidity was really stable and as we walked together we chatted about life and I said to him: "Do you know what we're all up to, Dad? Do you see us?"

'"Yes, I know everything that goes on, Millie, and I'm very proud of you all," he replied with a smile.

'I didn't dare ask him about what he thought of my time as a pole dancer, though! I think this might have been one of the main reasons for me to see him, actually. When I first started stripping I always had "What would my dad think of this?" in the back of my mind. Maybe deep down I've been searching for some sort of approval from him and that's what this meeting in the dream was about. He didn't mind, though – he knew about it and was still proud of me.

'Then he showed me into a house and told me that he lived there now. It was in a row of houses near our house in real life. We went inside and he had a table ready for dinner out in the garden. He'd always loved eating outside. He'd cooked us paella – his favourite.

'The lucidity was still so stable and we were sitting outside talking about life and eating and then suddenly it became cloudy, the light changed and I knew it was coming to an end. I felt myself being pulled back to waking reality so I shouted, "Bye, Dad!" before I got sucked out of the dream and woke up in bed.'

Life since the dream: 'Now I'm thinking about it, as well as it being great to have met my dad again, I'm sure that meeting him in the lucid dream was a way for me to get his blessing on the way I chose to live my life. I know it's a lifestyle no father would really want his daughter to have, but in the dream he seemed so accepting and wasn't judgemental at all. He loved me regardless.

167

'Anyway, the pole dancing led to the photography career so it was all for the best in the end. It was nice to be able to let go of judgements though, and know that he loves me whatever path I take.'

Millie's dream is not only a moving example of interaction with the 1 per cent, but also of lucid dream healing, as it allowed her to let go of self-doubt and judgement and to make peace with herself. Also, her father was right to be proud of his daughter, as she is now one of the world's leading pole-dance photographers. Check out www.millierobson.com to see her work.

Making friends with the dream

As we learnt back in Chapter 1, lucid dreaming is all about making friends. It's not about manipulating the unconscious or controlling our dreams, it's about befriending our unconscious and extending the hand of friendship to our inner dreamer. The majority of our potential is stored in the unconscious mind and so if we can make friends with the unconscious we not only step into a creative power as yet untapped but, as I mentioned previously, we also make a very beneficial ally.

Carl Jung believed that the 'unconscious mind could be experienced as a living, numinous presence, a constant companion'[4], and that the pinnacle of psychological completion was to learn how to relate to the unconscious, how to know the unconscious and how to befriend the unconscious. And what's the best way to do this? Jung was unequivocal: by exploring our dreams.

If you engage dream work with this motivation then every time you write down a dream, every time you become lucid within a dream and every time you even *try* to become lucid within a dream you're sending a strong and definite message to your unconscious mind – one that says, 'I want to know you. I'm interested in what you're saying. I want to be friends.'

It's no coincidence that people start to feel more creative, more empowered and more whole when they begin working with their dreams. These are all side effects of making friends with the powerhouse of psychic energy that 'you' share your mind with.

This attitude of friendship towards our night-time dreams can be extended to include the shared dream of waking life. If we open ourselves to a sense of curiosity, interest and friendliness to the waking dream we may find that it responds in the same way that our unconscious does: the dream becomes more vivid, more insightful and more lucid.

Lucidity in the big dream

One of the concepts that I explore in depth in *Dreams of Awakening* is the concept of 'lucid living': being lucid in the big dream – the shared dream of waking life. In a beginner's guide such as this I'm wary of delving into the subject too deeply and yet it's an essential point to touch on as we approach the end of the book.

So what's lucid living all about? Once we establish a stabilized lucid dreaming practice, we're learning a new habit of recognition and of 'seeing through illusion' that can help us to become aware not only of our dream projections but also of our waking projections. This is how we begin to live lucidly, because we start to recognize our psychological projections in the same way as we recognize our dreams.

Carl Jung believed that the majority of our problems are caused by being unaware of our psychological projections. Projection has been described as 'a psychological defence mechanism in which we unconsciously project our own unacceptable qualities onto others.' But how does it work? By not knowing that we're projecting our blame onto others we needlessly create suffering for both them and us.

By not knowing that we're having others' expectations projected onto us we strive to please them while hurting ourselves. So if there were a practice that could directly help us to recognize projections, and to see them for what they are, wouldn't that be worth learning? Well, that practice is lucid dreaming and your learning has already begun.

The late Tibetan lama Traleg Rinpoche said that 'to recognize that you're dreaming while you're dreaming is a big step forward in your practice because you can use that same technique in your daily life too. This is the main teaching of dream yoga: to learn how to recondition the mind in this way. If we do this through the practice of dream yoga it encourages us to be more spontaneous... more creative, more positive.'[5]

When I was 16 I didn't get into lucid dreaming to become more aware, I got into it for fun. But after a couple of years of messing around in the playground of my mind I started to see the world a bit differently. I couldn't forget the experiences of my lucid dreams, and even though I was mainly using them for sex and skateboarding I was becoming aware that I was skateboarding around my mind and that I was gaining access to the very fabric of my consciousness while I slept.

What if I could gain access to the fabric of waking reality too? Could I find a way to bring the manifestational power of the lucid dream state into the waking state? Questions like this began to come up again and again. This was compounded when, at 19, I started looking at Tibetan Buddhism and its concepts of the dreamlike nature of waking reality.

And so began a new chapter of my lucid dream training, one that eventually led me to engage in a lifetime project of waking up, stepping out of self-deception, and finding a way to move beyond the seeming limitations of life. For as we learn to wake up in our dreams, we start to wake up in our lives.

One woman whom I witnessed first-hand enter into an experience of lucid living was Ester, a jazz singer from Brazil who told me of a lucid dream that not only brought tears to my eyes as I read it but left me with a feeling that this dreamer had changed forever, entering into a raised vibration of lucid living that seemed to have affected her at a very deep level.

Case study: Fear of death, and lucid living

Dreamer: *Ester, Brazil*

Age: *31*

The lowdown from Ester: *'I'd been asking the Holy Spirit, the higher energy – whatever you want to call it – for advice about what to experience in my next lucid dream. I asked for anything that would help me in my spiritual path. I could never have expected what happened, though.'*

Ester's dream report: *'That same night I started having recurring dreams that I was going to die, but every time the moment of my death came I became lucid and then either I woke myself up or changed the dream. I didn't want to die – even though I knew it was a dream, it felt so real and I was afraid of death. I had these dreams for three nights, each time faced by death and each time becoming lucid and changing the dream.*

'Then, one evening while I was meditating, I realized something. The Holy Spirit wanted me to die in a lucid dream because I asked it to show me what would help me on the spiritual path! So before I went to sleep that night I told the universe that I was ready for this.

'That was the night it happened. I dreamed that I was in a car with a guy who wanted to harm me. We left the car and he killed me. But as I lay there dying I began to feel such love for him and I saw this amazing, beautiful light coming in my direction. It was brighter than the sun and suddenly my body disappeared into that light and I realized that the light was everything that had ever existed. The light was everything.

'I became the light and felt how it was constantly expanding. The light was infinite. There wasn't any

thought, feeling, or sensation; I wasn't a body anymore. There was no separation, no need of being something else, no need for the mind, and no need for time or perception.

'*The light was everything there ever was and it was nothing at the same time. This light was forever, expanding itself constantly, peacefully. Everything was light and I had become the light. I don't know how long this lasted. Then, suddenly, a very tiny idea of a world apart from that light seemed to appear, and I saw the world appearing again like a video game being reloaded. In an instant I was awake, in my bed, but the light was still with me, filling up the room.*'

Life since the dream: '*Ah, Charlie, since that dream I've been flying! Now I know that nothing can be apart from God! We are divine energy! We are inseparable, now as one. It's hard to say in words but I feel now that this life is a dream and that our experience of this body is a dream. We remain forever part of the light. We never left home. We were always safe.*

'*Since that dream, now that I know the truth, it's amazing how easy it is to forgive the things that used to affect me. I live as if I'm lucid. It's so easy to talk to the universe, to get back to nature. Love remains so strongly in me.*

'*Every moment of my life now is like a lucid dream. I see that we're awakening in the dream together. Lucid dreaming has expanded my mind and I'm very happy for it coming into my life. Going to your workshops has opened a door for me. I've started to feel lucid in my everyday life, seeing life as an energetic form, just like my dreams.*

'I look at people now and wonder how such beauty could appear so limited. Lucid dreaming is actually expanding my mind into a higher consciousness while I'm awake. And for this I'm very happy.'

Ester experienced a truly life-changing lucid dream that exemplifies just how profound our lucid dream training can be, and how the phrase 'just a dream' is so strongly negated once we become fully conscious within our dreams and commune with the divine potential that resides within.

Lucid living doesn't mean we lose touch with reality and think that life doesn't matter because it's all a dream anyway. It means quite the opposite, in fact – it means that we reconnect fully with the shared, dreamlike experience of waking life and start treating every other person, creature and thing as we would in our lucid dreams, with acceptance, friendliness and kindness.

There's one man who has explored this concept of lucid living more than most; in fact he even wrote a book about it. He's the author of over 30 books on gnostic philosophy, the world's religions and how to be more awake in everyday life. He's an embodiment of his teachings, and he also has a wonderful surname.

Tips from the pros: Lucid living, with Tim Freke

Pay attention to the paradox of your identity

When you dream lucidly you appear to be a character in your dream, but you're also conscious of being the dreamer; you know you're the awareness within which the dream is arising.

Lucid living is similar but occurs in the waking state. If you want to live lucidly be conscious of the character you appear to be in the life-dream, and also of your deeper identity as awareness within which all your experiences are arising.

Be the I-witness

To become conscious of your deeper identity as awareness move your attention from the sensations and thoughts you're experiencing to the 'I' of awareness, which is the experiencer witnessing this moment. This can seem tricky because the 'I-witness' is formless. It has no shape or colour. It makes no noise. The 'I' of awareness can't be known as an object within your experience, because it's the subject of all you're experiencing. It can't be seen because it is awareness that is experiencing looking. It can't be heard because it is awareness that is experiencing listening. Awareness can't be known as an *object* within your experience, because it is the *subject* of all you are experiencing.

If you want to live lucidly become conscious of being the formless presence of awareness that is witnessing all that you're experiencing right now.

See that you're both separate and not-separate

In a dream you appear to be a separate individual among other separate individuals. Yet if you dream lucidly you see that they are all manifestations of your deeper identity as the dreamer. From this perspective you're one with everything and everyone in your dream.

If you want to live lucidly be conscious in the waking state that you're also separate and not-separate from others and the world. You appear to be a separate individual within the dream of life, but as awareness you're one with all that's arising within the life-dream.

There's often the assumption that once we experience oneness the separateness will disappear, but this is not the case. As in a lucid dream the oneness and the separateness coexist. Allow the paradoxical possibility of being both separate and not-separate at the same time and see what happens.

Philosopher Tim Freke is the author of *Lucid Living* and runs experiential retreats internationally. See www. TheMysteryExperience.com for more information.

Conclusion

As this book is a beginner's guide, we haven't explored many of the more advanced implications of lucid dreaming – in relation to the spiritual path, the nature of reality and out-of-body experiences – but if you want to take your exploration further, do check out my first book, *Dreams of Awakening*, which offers a more comprehensive and far-reaching journey into lucid dreaming on the spiritual path.

However, in this introductory guide we've laid a solid foundation for your lucid dream training and you now have a fully stocked toolbox of techniques that contains everything you need to be a lucid dreamer.

We sleep for a third of our lives, but are awake for two-thirds of it, so if lucid dreaming doesn't directly affect the time that we spend awake then maybe it's not such a big deal after all? But it *does* change our waking lives and I've seen it change thousands of people's lives for the better. Just think of the huge changes that have been made by the subjects of our case studies: curing nicotine addiction, choosing a new career path, embracing the shadow, healing kidney disease, letting go of judgement and waking up to a spiritual breakthrough.

The defining characteristic of each one of those people was not that they are especially talented lucid dreamers but that they opened themselves up to a possibility that their dreams were more powerful than they'd ever imagined. They wanted to 'see beyond the well' – just like the frog from toolbox 1.

Essentially, I see the lucid dream state as a laboratory of self-development in which we train in our dreams to help engage the shared dream of waking life with more lucid awareness. What you do in your lucid dreams can create major psychological shifts that affect your waking life in remarkable ways.

Over the past year, as I have been writing this book, I've had the privilege to work with people who are using lucid dreaming to really push the boundaries of healing and psychological development. One young man who hears voices in his head has used his lucid dreams to actually meet up with personifications of these voices, and integrate and befriend them, which has led to a significant decrease in the frequency and negative tone of the voices. Another young man approaching death from cancer is using lucid dream training to prepare himself for his coming death. A quadriplegic friend of mine has been using his lucid dreams to do all the things his body can't do anymore: running, swimming and mountain biking. And an ex-soldier who came on one of my retreats has said that he felt he had integrated more of his psychological baggage in a 4-day lucid dreaming retreat than he had in years of therapy. We are barely scratching the surface of what is possible through lucid dreaming.

At my workshops I always say: 'The greatest benefits of lucid dreaming come not in the dreamtime but in the daytime,' as our psyche integrates the changes we make in the lucid dream state into our waking mind. But how does this work exactly? Every time you fly through the sky in a lucid dream you're creating a new habit of mind that'll allow you to fly beyond your limitations in the waking state. Every time you walk through a wall in a lucid dream you're implanting a revolutionary new possibility into your psyche that says, 'what seems to be solid is not always so'. Every time you integrate and embrace your shadow and inner demons in the lucid dream you're creating new perspectives which will make it easier to face the 'demons' of self-doubt and fear in your everyday life.

On top of that, lucid dreaming helps you to get to know yourself better, and once you know yourself better you can better help yourself to be a kinder and more beneficial person. Also, by getting to know your own psychology you're getting to know the psychology of others and so become better equipped to help them too.

We soon learn that we're all in this together – dreamers in the same dream – and that everybody is trying their best, however flawed their best may seem. So, let's make friends with the other dream characters and with the Great Dreamer: the Universal Mind that dreams this shared dream into being.

My hope is that by reading this book, which has simply touched upon the huge and important subject of lucid dreaming, you too have been helped to 'see beyond the well' and are now able to appreciate just how powerful the lucid dreaming mind can be.

So dream on, dreamer, and keep moving fearlessly towards the ocean, knowing that the time has come to leave the well and to see the oceanic vastness of your own potential. Follow your dreams, they know the way ...

References

Introduction

1. http://www.bbc.co.uk/news/health-11741350

Chapter 1

1. http://www.ncbi.nlm.nih.gov/pmc/articles/PMC2737577/

2. Max-Planck-Gesellschaft (July 27, 2012). Lucid dreamers help scientists locate the seat of meta-consciousness in the brain.

3. DeYoung C.G., Hirsh J.B., Shane M.S., Papademetris X., Rajeevan N. and Gray J.R. 'Testing predictions from personality neuroscience' (June 2010). *Psychological Science* 21(6): 820–828. doi:10.1177/09567610370159. PMC 3049165. PMID 20435951.

4. http://www.ncbi.nlm.nih.gov/pmc/articles/PMC3707083/

5. Activity within the dorsolateral prefrontal cortex ceases entirely during REM sleep.

6. Rob Nairn, Tara Rokpa Centre Christmas retreat, 2013

7. LaBerge, S. 'Lucid dreaming: Evidence and methodology' (2000), *Behavioral and Brain Sciences* 23 (6): 962–3. doi:10.1017/S0140525X00574020

8. http://www.nih.gov/news/health/oct2013/ninds-17.htm

9. http://dreamstudies.org/2009/09/18/lucid-dreaming-hybrid-gamma-biurnal-beats/

10. I should actually change this bit because in early 2014 I had a series of three lucid dreams in which I intentionally sent healing energy to my eyes by using the Buddhist mantra of the medicine

Buddha. At the point of writing, I no longer need to wear my glasses and my eyesight has improved dramatically.

11. http://www.livescience.com/6521-video-gamers-control-dreams-study-suggests.html

12. In a 2012 BBC *Horizon* documentary called 'How Big is the Unconscious Mind' several of the scientists believed that it was more like 95 per cent to 5 per cent in favour of the unconscious.

13. Lama Surya Das, *Dream Yoga*, Sounds True audio

14. Anthony Stevens, *Jung: A Very Short Introduction*, (Oxford University Press, 2001), p.82

Chapter 2

1. http://www.sciencedaily.com/releases/2007/06/070614085118.htm

2. Tholey, P. 1990

3. Erlacher D. and Schredl M. 'Cardiovascular Responses to Dreamed Physical Exercise During REM Lucid Dreaming' (2008)

4. Behncke L., 'Mental Skills training for sports: a brief review' Athletic Insight: The Online Journal of Sports Psychology, March 2004.

5. http://www.telegraph.co.uk/news/worldnews/northamerica/usa/1363146/Thinking-about-exercise-can-beef-up-biceps.html

6. Tholey P. (1981)

7. Tholey P. (1990)

8. Erlacher D. Stumbrys. T., Heidelberg University, Germany; University of Bern, Switzerland and Schredl, M., Central Institute of Mental Health, Mannheim, Germany. 'Frequency of lucid dreams and lucid dream practice in German athletes, imagination, cognitions and personality'. Vol. 31(3) 237-246, 2011-2012

9. *New Scientist*, December 21/28 2013, UK edition.

10. Michael Katz, *Tibetan Dream Yoga* (Bodhi Tree 2011), p.31

11. Sleep scientists used to speak of five stages of sleep, but in 2007 the American Academy of Sleep Medicine decided to group stages 3 and 4 together, so there are now four stages.

Chapter 3

1. Rob Nairn, Tara Rokpa Centre Christmas retreat, 2013.

2. Paul and Charla Devereux, *Lucid Dreaming: Accessing Your Inner Virtual Realities* (Daily Grail Publishing, 2011), p.13

3. Jill Bolte Taylor, PhD, *My Stroke of Insight* (Hodder and Stoughton, 2008), p.30

4. Amit Goswami, in conversation with the author, 2008.

5. Paul and Charla Devereux, *Lucid Dreaming: Accessing Your Inner Virtual Realities* (Daily Grail Publishing, 2011), p.115

6. Daniel Love, *Are you Dreaming*? (Enchanted Loom Publishing, 2013), p.2

Chapter 4

1. David Richo, *Shadow Dance, Liberating the Power and Creativity of Your Dark Side* (Shambhala, 1999), p.14

2. Cicchetti, J. 'Archetypes and the Collective Unconscious', http://www.hahnemanninstituut.nl/admin/uploads/pdf/ Archetypes.pdf

3. ibid.

4. Jung didn't use the term 'higher self', instead he used a capital S to distinguish between the self of everyday usage (which refers to ego or persona) and the concept of the Self, which transcends the ego and represents the highest psychological completeness. However, my experience is that people often forget this so I use the term 'higher self' when I talk of self with a capital S.

5. http://psychology.about.com/od/personalitydevelopment/tp/ archetypes.htm

6. Paul and Charla Devereux, *Lucid Dreaming: Accessing Your Inner Virtual Realities* (Daily Grail Publishing, 2011), p.105

7. Anthony Stevens, *Jung: A Very Short Introduction*, (Oxford University Press, 2001), p.56

8. Paul and Charla Devereux, *Lucid Dreaming: Accessing Your Inner Virtual Realities* (Daily Grail Publishing, 2011), p.92

9. C.G. Jung, *The Archetypes and the Collective Unconscious (The Collected Works of C.G Jung, Vol 9. Part 1)* (Routledge and Kegan Paul, 1959)

10. Zadra A.L., Pihl R.O. 'Lucid dreaming as a treatment for recurrent nightmares'. http://www.ncbi.nlm.nih.gov/pubmed/8996716

11. http://www.ncbi.nlm.nih.gov/pubmed/8996716

12. Lucid dreaming treatment for nightmares: a pilot study. Spoormaker VI1, van den Bout J. 2006 http://www.ncbi.nlm.nih.gov/pubmed/17053341

13. European Science Foundation. 'New Links Between Lucid Dreaming And Psychosis Could Revive Dream Therapy In Psychiatry.' *ScienceDaily*, 29 July 2009. www.sciencedaily.com/releases/2009/07/090728184831.htm

14. Paul and Charla Devereux, *Lucid Dreaming: Accessing Your Inner Virtual Realities* (Daily Grail Publishing, 2011), p.18

15. Michael Katz, *Tibetan Dream Yoga* (Bodhi Tree, 2011), p.67, commenting on Gyaltrul Rinpoche, *Ancient Wisdom* (Snow Lion Publications, 1993), p.80

16. www.lucidity.com/luciddreamingFAQ2.html

17. B. Alan Wallace, *Dreaming Yourself Awake: Lucid Dreaming and Tibetan Dream Yoga for Insight and Transformation* (Shambhala Publications, 2012), p.30

18. www.lucidity.com/NL63.RU.Naps.html

Chapter 5

1. http://dreamstudies.org/history-of-lucid-dreaming-ancient-india-to-the-enlightenment/

2. Paul and Charla Devereux, *Lucid Dreaming: Accessing Your Inner Virtual Realities* (Daily Grail Publishing, 2011), p.25

3. Paul and Charla Devereux, *Lucid Dreaming: Accessing Your Inner Virtual Realities* (Daily Grail Publishing, 2011), p.29

4. Paul and Charla Devereux, *Lucid Dreaming: Accessing Your Inner Virtual Realities* (Daily Grail Publishing, 2011), p.30

5. Paul and Charla Devereux, *Lucid Dreaming: Accessing Your Inner Virtual Realities* (Daily Grail Publishing, 2011), p.32

6. Paul and Charla Devereux, *Lucid Dreaming: Accessing Your Inner Virtual Realities* (Daily Grail Publishing, 2011), p.33

7. http://dreamstudies.org/history-of-lucid-dreaming-ancient-india-to-the-enlightenment/

8. Paul and Charla Devereux, *Lucid Dreaming: Accessing Your Inner Virtual Realities* (Daily Grail Publishing, 2011), p.36

9. *New Scientist,* UK edition, December 2013, p.22

10. Richard Wiseman *Nightschool*, 2014, p.22

11. ibid., p.24

12. Paul and Charla Devereux, *Lucid Dreaming: Accessing Your Inner Virtual Realities* (Daily Grail Publishing, 2011), p.71

13. ibid., p.76

Chapter 6

1. Rinpoche (pronounced like cabaret) is a Tibetan word meaning 'precious' and is used as a title for esteemed Tibetan teachers.

2. Bardo is a Sanskrit word that means 'place in between'. The after-death bardo state is the place in between this life and the next.

3. http://www.bbc.co.uk/religion/religions/islam/subdivisions/sufism_1.shtml

4. Paul and Charla Devereux, *Lucid Dreaming: Accessing Your Inner Virtual Realities* (Daily Grail Publishing, 2011), p.61

5. Paul and Charla Devereux, *Lucid Dreaming: Accessing Your Inner Virtual Realities* (Daily Grail Publishing, 2011), p.31

6. Paul and Charla Devereux, *Lucid Dreaming: Accessing Your Inner Virtual Realities* (Daily Grail Publishing, 2011), p.32

7. http://www.islamicacademy.org/html/Dua/How_to_do_Istakhara.htm

Chapter 7

1. Effects of pyridoxine on dreaming: a preliminary study. Ebben M, Lequerica A, Spielman A. http://www.ncbi.nlm.nih.gov/pubmed/11883552

2. ibid.

3. I have a mix that contains 60 per cent raw hemp seed powder, 10 per cent wheatgrass powder, 10 per cent raw cacao powder, 10 per cent purple maca root powder, 10 per cent spirulina powder and a big pinch of turmeric, which gives a huge boost of B vitamins, amino acids, magnesium and zinc that gives the body all it needs to stay lucid. Mix with water or juice and have a big

glass in the morning to stay lucid all day, or a late-night dose to stay lucid at night!

4. http://www.medicalnewstoday.com/releases/163169.php

5. http://www.iofbonehealth.org/calcium-rich-foods

6. http://www.huffingtonpost.co.uk/marek-doyle/help-me-sleep-magnesium-secret-to-sleep-problems_b_3311795.html

7. http://www.telegraph.co.uk/health/elderhealth/9979776/Shakespeare-was-right-rosemary-oil-boosts-memory.html

8. Paul and Charla Devereux, *Lucid Dreaming: Accessing Your Inner Virtual Realities* (Daily Grail Publishing, 2011), p.99

9. http://www.sciencedaily.com/releases/2008/09/080921162021.htm

10. http://www.cell.com/current-biology/retrieve/pii/S0960982213007549

11. http://science.time.com/2013/07/25/how-the-moon-messes-with-your-sleep/

Chapter 8

1. http://drdavidhamilton.com/think-yourself-well-scientific-evidence-for-the-power-of-visualisation/

2. Michael Katz, *Tibetan Dream Yoga* (Bodhi Tree, 2011), p.31.

3. In 2012 a team of researchers from ATR Computational Neuroscience Laboratories in Kyoto, Japan, used functional neuroimaging to scan the brains of three people as they slept and managed to monitor changes in activity that could then be related to the content of their dreams. When we dream about or visualize a certain object our brains generate a unique neural pattern. By painstakingly charting these patterns for hundreds of objects the scientists were able to decode the images of the dream with 60 per cent accuracy. http://www.nature.com/news/scientists-read-dreams-1.116255.

4. Anthony Stevens, *Jung: A Very Short Introduction*, (Oxford University Press, 2001), p.38

5. Traleg Rinpoche, *Dream Yoga* DVD set, E-Vam Buddhist Institute

Acknowledgements

With this book coming so soon after *Dreams of Awakening* I'd assumed there might be fewer people to thank, but in fact there are perhaps even more!

Firstly I'd like to thank all the contributors: Rob Nairn, Robert Waggoner, Daniel Love, Ryan Hurd, Clare Johnson, Luigi Sciambarella, Tim Freke, Keith Hearne, Lama Yeshe Rinpoche, Sergio Magaña, Nigel Hamilton, John Lockley and Stanley Krippner.

Although there have been many people who've contributed to this book, I take full responsibility for any errors or inaccuracies within the text, and I apologize for any and all of these.

Thanks to all those who kindly read through sections of the various drafts and offered corrections and advice, including Robert Waggoner (thanks so much for the advice), Rob Nairn, Albert Buhr, Melanie Schädlich, Daniel Love, Violet Lim and Nick Begley.

Special thanks to the case study subjects – Antonio, Nina, Kerri, Bruno, Millie and Ester – for being so kind and courageous in sharing your experiences.

Thanks to Debra Wolter for the tireless editing work, and Michelle, Amy, Jo, Ruth, Jessica, Duncan, Tom, Julie and the rest of the brilliant team at Hay House for all their hard work. Probably the best publisher to work for in the world.

To my teachers, Lama Yeshe Rinpoche, Rob Nairn, the late Akong Rinpoche, Sogyal Rinpoche, the late Mervyn Minall-Jones and Lama Zangmo, for their kindness and patience with me.

To the London Samye Dzong Buddhist Centre sangha, with whom I have lived for the past four years, and to all those who choose to take the road less travelled.

To the Mindfulness Association for their continued support, Ya'Acov Darling Khan for guidance, Gateways of the Mind, Sergio Magaña for the world tour, Albert Buhr for the massages, the THROWDOWN community that I think of every day, and all my dear friends.

Huge thanks to my mum, dad, brother and family, who have continued to support me. And to my fiancée Jade, for keeping me grounded with her Northernness.

Thanks to all the people I've had the pleasure of teaching lucid dreaming to around the world, and finally, thanks to you for reading this book. I wish you full lucidity in both your waking and dream lives!

Permissions

Polygraph image p.112: Hearne, K. (1978) *Lucid dreams – an electrophysiological and psychological study*. PhD thesis. University of Liverpool, England. Submitted May, 1978 (p.163).

Index

ABOUT THE AUTHOR

Charlie Morley has been a self-taught lucid dreamer since the age of 17 and a practising Buddhist for the past 12 years, after taking refuge with Akong Rinpoche. In 2008, at the age of 25, Charlie started teaching lucid dreaming within the context of Tibetan Buddhism at the request of his mentor, the well-known meditation instructor Rob Nairn.

Soon after he started teaching, Charlie received the traditional Tibetan Buddhist 'authorization to teach' from his teacher, Lama Yeshe Rinpoche, which was not only a great honour but also a valuable seal of approval from such a highly regarded lama.

In 2010, Charlie and Rob Nairn began to pioneer a new holistic approach to lucid dreaming and conscious sleeping called Mindfulness of Dream & Sleep. Since then Charlie has run lucid dreaming workshops and Mindfulness of Dream & Sleep retreats around the UK, Europe, Africa and America. He was featured on BBC Radio 4, and lectured at Goldsmiths University, London, Cape Town Medical School and the Royal Geographical Society. In 2011, he gave the first ever TED talk on lucid dreaming at a conference in San Diego.

Before being asked to teach lucid dreaming, Charlie had completed a BA honours degree in drama, which led him to work as an actor, a scriptwriter and even a rapper in a Buddhist hip-hop group. He currently lives at Kagyu Samye Dzong Buddhist Centre in London with his fiancée, Jade. He has a 1st Dan blackbelt in kickboxing and enjoys films, surfing and dreaming!

www.charliemorley.com

Notes

Notes

Notes

Notes

Notes

Notes

Notes

Notes

HAY HOUSE

Look within

Join the conversation about latest products,
events, exclusive offers and more.

f Hay House UK

🐦 @HayHouseUK

📷 @hayhouseuk

💜 healyourlife.com

We'd love to hear from you!